REA

ACPL ITEM
DISCARDED

P9-BIL-920

Creating a Power Web Site

HTML, TABLES, IMAGEMAPS, FRAMES, AND FORMS

By **Gail Junion-Metz** and **Brad Stephens**

Neal-Schuman Publishers, Inc.
New York   London

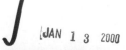
JAN 1 3 2000

Published by Neal-Schuman Publishers, Inc.
100 Varick Street
New York, NY 10013

Copyright © 1998 by Gail Junion-Metz and Brad Stephens

All rights reserved. Reproduction of this book, in whole or in part, without written permission of the publisher is prohibited.

Printed and bound in the United States of America

Library of Congress Cataloging-in-Publication Data

Junion-Metz, Gail, 1947–
    Creating a power web site : HTML, tables, imagemaps, frames, and
    forms / Gail Junion-Metz, Brad Stephens.
        p.   cm.
    Includes bibliographical references and index.
    ISBN 1–56576–323–2
1. Web sites—Design. 2. Library information networks. 3. Web
sites—United States—Design. 4. Library information networks—
United States. I. Stephens, Brad. II. Title.
Z674.75.W67J88   1998
005.7'2—dc21   98–38806
                                                        CIP

Contents

Acknowledgments

Brad would like to thank his wife, Cara, and family for all their encouragement and patience. Gail would like to thank her husband, Ray, who has been through this before, for his understanding and support.

We would both like to thank the following people who helped us complete the book. Charles Ormsby, for help with the graphics; Carol Roddy, for permission to use selected OPLIN graphics; Christopher Adams and the folks at Boutell.Com, for permission to include an evaluation copy of the *Mapedit* software; Steven E. Brenner, for permission to include the PERL routines script; and the folks at the Free Software Foundation, for creating and providing permission to include both the Windows/NT and UNIX/Linux PERL interpreter. Finally, we'd like to thank Charles Harmon for his patience (and tenacity) in making sure the book meets the needs of librarians everywhere.

Figures

What's on the CD-ROM?

The CD-ROM contains four folders:

- The first folder, HTML, contains copies of most of the tagging examples illustrated in the book. It also contains copies of the HTML documents that have corresponding PERL scripts. All HTML files are saved as "plain text," so all you have to do to view them is insert the CD-ROM into your computer, fire up a graphical browser, like Netscape or Internet Explorer, and open up one of the "local" HTML files on the CD-ROM. (Remember: Your browser options control both the font types and sizes of all pages you view, so the image you see on your computer screen will probably differ from the HTML images printed in the book.)

- The second folder, PERL, contains copies of the PERL scripts that have corresponding HTML files. It also contains a file that contains important PERL commands. (You will want to save this file to your Web server's CGI-BIN directory.) All PERL scripts are saved as "plain text." To view them, use a word processor like Word or WordPerfect. (If you attempt to launch them from Microsoft Explorer, "select" your word processing software from the applications window.) Copy them "as is" or modify them and store them on your Web server (with .pl file extensions).

- The third folder, PROGRAMS, contains two versions of the PERL interpreter software, one for Windows/NT and one for Linux/UNIX. (Be sure to install the correct version on your Web Server!) It also contains an evaluation copy of the *Mapedit* software. Win_Perl and *Mapedit* have been "unzipped" and are ready to be used. (Be sure to read the "readme" files and manuals if you want to start using them correctly or install them on your Web server or computer's hard-drive.) Unix_perl is saved on the disk as a tar.gz file. It will have to be "unzipped" before you install it on your server.

- The fourth folder, TEXT, contains simple installation instructions for the *Mapedit* software.

Hint: If you load the sample PERL scripts into a test directory on your Web server, you can get the HTML sample files and the PERL scripts to interact with each other, just like they will in real life.

CD-ROM INDEX

HTML

PERL

PROGRAMS

TEXT

List of "Test Your Knowledge" Topics

Preface

Contrary to popular perception, just because a Web site uses animation and sound, doesn't mean it's a "power" Web site. Powerful Web sites are, instead, ones that are carefully planned to anticipate their intended users' needs and to meet them as efficiently as possible. They are well-organized, interactive, and informative—much like first-rate libraries. Like first-rate libraries, powerful library Web sites use automated techniques and superb design to deliver information and services.

We wrote *Creating a Power Web Site: HTML, Tables, Frames, and Forms* to help librarians learn the techniques and skills they need to upgrade their Web sites as quickly and as easily as possible. We do this by taking common library services—such as reserving materials, requesting interlibrary loans, and registering for library cards—and showing you how to make these services more convenient for patrons by offering them through your library's Web site. Adapting these and other services for the Web requires some additional HTML techniques (imagemaps, frames, and tables); interactivity (library users supply information on forms and your Web site responds automatically and appropriately); and learning how to use a fairly simple programming language called PERL. Thanks to today's publishing technologies, in addition to explaining how to do it, we were also able to include a CD-ROM with ready-to-load (or adapt) forms you can put on your own Web site. Once you've designed or adapted one service for the Web using a combination of these techniques, you'll be able—and eager—to add more and more information and services to your Web site. And then you'll have a power Web site!

SCOPE

There are many books available in bookstores (and probably on your own library shelves) on Web site design and techniques. *Creating a Power Web Site* and the CD-ROM found in the back of this book, though, are specifically designed for libraries. All of the examples, sample scripts, forms, and exercises are library-related. They make it possible for you to:

- Quickly upgrade the look of your whole Web Site using the examples and programming referred to in the text and viewable/usable via the CD-ROM.
- Start using HTML 3.2 tags (and the various additional attributes that come along

with the tags) to arrange and display text and graphics on your library's Web pages in a more sophisticated manner.

- Create image maps quickly and easily using the *Mapedit* software included on the CD-ROM.
- Create simple tables for your Web pages, which will 1) save space, 2) look better than regular lists of text, and 3) provide a visual change-of-pace for visitors to your Web site.
- Create simple frames to divide your Web pages, as well as create navigational frames that can serve as directories/maps to your whole Web site.
- Create both HTML forms and PERL scripts. We include real examples in the text and on the CD-ROM that you can use either "as is" or modify to match your specific needs. We've also included PERL programs that will help you start writing your own first scripts.

Because the most productive place to practice your new skills is on your own library's Web site, we've included several different versions of the PERL interpreter software on the CD-ROM. So, no matter what type of Web server your library uses, you can start writing PERL scripts without having to search the Web for the correct program and download it. The CD-ROM also includes a free evaluation copy of the nifty imagemap program called *Mapedit*. Using it, you can create imagemaps for your Web pages almost as fast as you can scan the graphics themselves. See page xi for a complete description of the CD-ROM's contents.

Our goal was to put together a book and CD-ROM package that you could use as a "one-stop" resource for upgrading your library's Web site without having to start from scratch, FTP anything from anywhere, or read lots of the technobabble so common to Internet books (most of which seem written more for computer geeks than for librarians with limited time and patience).

Many library users have limited access to Web sites because they use older equipment that requires them to use text-based browsers. Most libraries must design their Web sites carefully so that the largest possible number of patrons using different computers and different Web browsers can visit and easily view it. HTML tagging is changing rapidly. Many of the new tags and attributes included in HTML4 are not currently accessible using the browser versions (Netscape 2+, 3+, and Microsoft Internet Explorer 2+ and 3+) found on most library and home computers. Because of these practicalities, we decided to cover HTML tags and attributes only through HTML 3.2, even though such coverage excludes stylesheets and other dynamic HTML features. We feel that this decision gives you the tools you need to create an upgraded, yet accessible, Web site that will work well for most in-house and remote users.

If you're not the person who will actually upgrade your library's Web site, but you must converse with (and understand) the person who will, you can use *Creating a Power Web Site* to provide you with the necessary background information you need to work with your "techies" and speak a little of their language.

ORGANIZATION

We have tried to take a simple, practical approach to some complex topics. For example, instead of discussing each and every HTML 2, 3.0, and 3.2 tag and attribute in detail, we discuss the tags you'll most likely find useful and have leave out the more esoteric ones (like the tags used for mathematical formulas). We have also tried to provide you with just enough information about each tag and attribute so that you'll be able to use it but not so much that you'll get confused. When we chose examples for tables, frames, and forms, and HTML/PERL scripts, we tried to choose ones from which you could build any number of variants that would suit your library's specific needs.

The chapters in *Creating a Power Web Site* are arranged in the order of the skills and tools you need to learn so you can upgrade your library's Web site:

Chapter 1 provides you with basic information about HTML, HTML editing programs, and some very basic design considerations.

Chapter 2 provides you with information and tips about the most-often used HTML 3.2 tags and attributes. It also contains library-based tagging examples, which are available both in the text and on the CD-ROM.

Chapter 3 gets you started creating imagemaps quickly and simply using the *Mapedit* program.

Chapter 4 covers the basics of table creation and provides you with a challenging exercise to test how well you learned table building.

Chapter 5 teaches you how to build frames for your Web pages and how to get different frames to work together on a Web site. (Try the "live" frames documents on the CD-ROM!)

Chapter 6 introduces you to building HTML forms and the different table input elements you can use to create customized forms for your Web pages.

Chapter 7 provides you with four commonly used library forms that you can use "as is" or customize locally. (Check out the CD-ROM for the HTML files.)

Chapter 8 introduces you gently and simply to the PERL programming language. It outlines the various types of PERL commands and functions that are most common to CGI scripts. It also explains how CGI scripts handle HTML data. Finally, it provides you with sample HTML forms and corresponding PERL script, so you can see how the two compare and interact with each other. All through this chapter you'll find lots of exercise opportunities to test your knowledge of PERL.

Chapter 9 continues to build on the PERL you learned in Chapter 8. It also contains five interactive HTML form/PERL script pairs that you can study (or try out on the Web) as well as use (or modify) locally.

Appendix A is a non-technical, easy-to-understand glossary of general Web terms, as well as terms unique to HTML and PERL.

Appendix B contains references to a selected list of the latest books and Web sites related to chapter topics.

Appendix C lists the most commonly used HTML equivalent characters, so you can add symbols and diacritical marks to your Web pages that don't show up on your computer's keyboard.

Appendix D lists browser-safe hexadecimal color codes, so that you can create colored backgrounds, text, and links on your Web pages easily.

Appendix E is a PERL command "cheat sheet" that you will want to use when trying to write your first PERL script (and many PERL scripts after that).

Because it's important that you grasp the concepts presented in one chapter before moving on to the next, we've included short but important special sections called "What You've Learned So Far" and "Test Your Knowledge" throughout the book. We encourage you to use these as guideposts to help you assess your understanding before moving on to the next section.

Upgrading your library's Web site can be one of the most visible contributions you'll ever have a chance to make on the job. We hope you'll find *Creating a Power Web Site* makes the process less daunting and more enjoyable.

1

Introducing HTML

WHAT IS HTML?

HTML is short for Hypertext Markup Language. Before we discuss HTML document structure, let's first take a look at the two big concepts that make up HTML: hypertext and markup language. *Hypertext* enables you to jump from place to place around the Internet using links that are created by specific HTML tags. HTML is a language specifically designed for labeling documents that will be stored on Net and Web servers and accessed electronically via hypertext links. A *markup language* sets up instructions within a document, to show what the document text means, what that text should do, or what it should look like. There are all kinds of markup languages. If you use WordPerfect you are probably familiar with the Reveal Codes feature that displays the markup commands that WordPerfect inserts into a document as you format it.

There are two general types of markup languages. The first type contains very specific instructions that indicate exactly how a document is to be formatted and displayed. These are called *physical markup languages* and are designed primarily for printing text. The second type of markup language does not prescribe how a document should look, but describes what each part of the document is, so that however it is displayed or printed the document will vary in terms of display, but not in terms of organization. This is called a *logical markup language*.

HTML is a logical markup language with a few physical markup commands thrown in. The reason HTML is primarily a logical language, is that there are both graphical and text-only browsers in use, all of which display HTML tags very differently. What is possible using a graphical browser is sometimes not available in a text-only environment where certain display options cannot be displayed. Different graphical browsers interpret and display HTML tags somewhat differently. If HTML was primarily a physical markup language, only users with browsers that could handle specific tag and attribute instructions would be able to view that Web page.

HTML is a subset of a more general logical markup language called SGML (Standard Generalized Markup Language). SGML is a language that defines the elements of other more specific markup languages. As such, SGML is quite large and complex, while HTML is simpler and has far fewer tags.

So, what does HTML do?

- HTML creates documents.
- HTML organizes the structure of Web documents.
- HTML lets you emphasize and format text in different ways to make it stand out from other text.
- HTML lets you create both internal hypertext links between Web documents and external hypertext links to other Web documents.
- HTML lets you create specific arrangements of text (e.g., forms, frames, and tables) so you can organize and display text in different ways.

HOW DO BROWSERS INTERACT WITH HTML DOCUMENTS?

When a visitor wants to visit your library's home page they probably either type in the URL for it, select your Web page from their bookmark list, or click on a hypertext link to it. Any of these three options sends a request to your Web server for a copy of your library home page's HTML document. After receiving the request, your Web server sends a copy of your HTML document back to visitor's Web browser. The browser's job then, is to receive your HTML document, interpret the HTML tags, and then display it to the person sitting in front of their computer screen.

How a Web page ultimately displays on a browser screen is a result of two factors: the HTML tagging and an individual browser's locally defined settings. HTML tags identify the content of Web documents so that browsers can format, arrange, and display that information. The locally defined options that a visitor can set up on their own Web browser (e.g., font type and size, page background color) can also profoundly affect how your library home page will display.

ADVANTAGES TO HTML

HTML documents are small, so they take up very little space on your server and transfer quickly from your server to a visitor's browser. HTML works with any Windows, MacOS, or UNIX computer that can run a Web browser as well as read and understand HTML documents. It is a relatively simple and easy-to-learn markup language. Many of the attributes for HTML tags can be used with more than one type of tag, so once you know how an attribute affects one tag, you know how it affects others. You can view both text and HTML tags while creating Web documents and while viewing them via your browser (using its Document Source feature). You can also learn HTML "by example" by connecting to other library Web pages and then viewing the HTML tags that created them.

WHAT ABOUT DIFFERENT HTML VERSIONS?

HTML was designed so that it could be added onto without disturbing the logic of the basic language. As such, new tags and attributes are being added all the time. Most of these new tags and attributes eventually appear in periodically updated "official" versions of HTML that comply with SGML standards. In between official versions, additional new tags and attributes are being created by the developers of the two most popular Web browsers, Netscape and Internet Explorer. Most, but not all, of these tags are compatible with SGML and will eventually become part of the next official HTML version.

First, you'll need to make decisions about HTML. If your library decides that you will only use an official version of HTML, that will definitely affect how you will build your Web site. If your library decides to also use some of the "unofficial" tags and attributes created by the Web browser folks (Netscape and Internet Explorer), then you'll have to test your Web documents thoroughly to make sure they work with all different types of browsers and computers.

Second, you'll need to discuss which version of HTML you want to use. Patrons with older equipment and text-only browsers or older graphical browser versions (Netscape 1.1) will have trouble viewing Web pages created with later versions of HTML, because neither their computer nor their browser is designed to display more recently added tags. Libraries need to create Web sites that are accessible to a large number of visitors who use a variety of browsers and computer equipment. As such, we recommend that, for now, your library stick to HTML versions at or HTML 3.2. The newest version of HTML, HTML 4, contains many tags and attributes that are not viewable using the browser versions (Netscape and Internet Explorer 2+, 3+) found in most libraries, schools, and homes. This will surely change in the future, but for now sticking with at least HTML 3.2 will ensure that a majority of the visitors to your Web site will be able to view and use the information you provide for them.

DISADVANTAGES TO HTML

Because HTML is a logical markup language that identifies what the text is, rather than telling browsers how to display it exactly, you lose some control over how your Web pages will display. For instance, a visitor to your Web page controls (via their browser) both its font style and font size. These, in turn, affect how graphics display, how text wraps, and how tables and forms display. With HTML 3.2, however, you have a wider range of tags and attributes that specify text and image placement, alignment, and white space. So, although you don't have total control over the way your Web pages display, using some of the additional HTML tags and attributes you can make more specific suggestions to browsers as to how you want your Web page to display.

Another disadvantage to HTML is that some formatting tricks that are simple to do using word processors or desktop publishing programs are not quite as simple using HTML. Tagging text to appear a certain way on a Web page is simple or complex, depending on what you are specifically trying to do. Sometimes just a tag pair will take care of it; other times, you will need to build a table or create separate Web frames to accomplish the desired arrangement of content.

The last disadvantage to HTML doesn't have really anything to do with HTML, but with the fact that HTML documents have to be compatible with a wide range of graphical and text-only browsers. As such, when you are writing HTML documents you must add text descriptions of graphical images (using the ALT= attribute) so that visitors who are using text-only browsers can read of description of the image they can't see. Having to write HTML documents for different browsers means that your HTML documents will be more complex than if they assumed every visitor to your Web site had the same abilities to view them. More complex or not, it is important that library Web sites be accessible and easily viewable by all types of browsers.

CREATING HTML DOCUMENTS

Before you start creating or upgrading your library Web site, we recommend you create a team of HTML authors, if you haven't done so already. Assuming that you have done the necessary planning and design work for your Web site, HTML document creation can be done relatively quickly. This, however, will depend on how many hours you have to spend and how complex your Web site will be. A lot of HTML authoring involves proofreading and tweaking tagged documents. Having HTML team members proof each other's documents can relieve boredom and eliminate most HTML and typographical errors.

Hint: Tabs and indents are ignored by browsers. However, using them will make HTML document structure more apparent and easier to update.

Before you start tagging documents, spend time planning HTML templates, so that tagging will be consistent from document to document. Decide whether tags will be in caps, lower case, or a mix. Decide also whether you'll use tabs and indents in documents. Lastly, decide on a naming scheme for all documents and agree on folder or directory names where draft and final versions of documents will be stored.

There are a number of ways you can create HTML documents. You can create the text first, using any word processing program that allows you to save text in ASCII format (ClarisWorks, Word, WordPerfect, even the generic Win95/98/NT Wordpad program). After you finish writing the text, you can add HTML tags by inserting them around the text, using the same word processing program.

You can also take text you've created a while ago and add HTML tags to it. This is a quick way to put documents on your Web site, but there's a problem with simply adding HTML tags to an existing document. People read Web documents differently than they do paper documents. When tagging an existing document, you can easily fall into the trap of adding tags but forget to change the document's format. Web pages should, as a rule, be shorter, less wordy, and contain information formatted specifically for viewing on the Web.

You can also use HTML editing programs to add tags to either pre-existing documents or to documents you create from scratch. HTML editing programs are more effective when you already know the basics of HTML tagging. If you are just learning HTML, we recommend you create your first couple of Web documents by creating the text first and then manually adding HTML tags to it, rather than using an HTML editing program. This keeps you focused on the HTML tags and the content of your Web site, rather than focusing on how to use your HTML editing program. Once you have the basics of tagging down and know what tags do and how they display on different browsers, then start using an HTML editing program to make writing and updating HTML documents more efficient.

CREATING THE TEXT FIRST

If you will be creating Web documents and are just using a word processor, write the text first. After you have finished writing the text, go back through the document, adding HTML tags and hypertext links as appropriate, inserting them into the text using your word processor. Then save the document, including either an .HTM or .HTML as the extension to the document file name (e.g., FOO.HTML, FOO.HTM).

If using an HTML tagging program, first write the text using your favorite word processor. If your word processor also includes an HTML tagging program, start it and add the appropriate tags by choosing from its menu or button options. If your word processor does not include an HTML tagging program, save your text document, open up a stand-alone HTML tagging program, retrieve the document, and add HTML tags to it using the program's menu options. When you are done, save the document and include either the .HTM or .HTML extension to the document's file name.

HTML DRAFT DOCUMENTS

Viewing draft HTML documents so you will know how they will look on the Web is simple. Just open up your Web browser and take a look. To do this, start your browser. Choose your browser's Open a Local File option. Select the directory/folder or drive where the draft document is located, select it, and take a look at it. If you like what you see, fine. If not, exit your browser and try using different tags or arrangements of text. Continue viewing and revising your document until it looks the way you want it to.

HTML EDITING PROGRAMS

There are four types of HTML editing programs:

- Tagging programs
- WYSIWYG programs
- Conversion programs
- Template programs

Tagging programs create HTML documents by allowing you to select specific HTML tags, which the program then inserts around specific pieces of text. Tagging programs are standard features found in newer word processor versions. If you are using an older word processor version that does not include a tagging program, there are stand-alone versions available on the Net for free via FTP. Tagging programs can help you create Web documents fast, because they remember all the details about each tag and insert them correctly.

WYSIWYG (which stands for "what you see is what you get") programs allow you to see what your page will look like as you create an HTML document. Some programs add tags to a document and then display the text as you would view it using your browser; other programs provide you with pre-tagged Web pages that you fill out and then view.

Conversion programs take text from different programs (word processors, spreadsheets) and convert it into HTML documents. One of the main advantages to using a conversion program is that you don't have to type in, or even select HTML tags for

Hint: Tweaking might be hard to do if you don't know HTML tagging because you rely too heavily on your conversion program.

text, the programs do that for you. One of the disadvantages of using a conversion program is that they don't always convert files correctly. You sometimes have to tweak a converted document to make it work or look right.

Template programs are the newest type of editing programs. You select a basic Web page template, add your text to it, click on a "Create My Page" button and you have a Web page tagged correctly and ready to add to your server. Template programs are fast and easy, but they also tend to create cookie-cutter style Web sites that look similar to thousands of others that were created using the same template. One way to use template programs effectively, though, is to create your own unique template, save it, and then use that template to quickly create the rest of your Web site.

There are many good HTML editing programs available as freeware and shareware on the Web (see Appendix B for Web sites and books that list them). You can also purchase commercial editing software at your local computer store. Check to see which editor will work best for your library.

HTML DOCUMENT STRUCTURE

TEXT AND TAGS

There are essentially two parts to an HTML document: text and tags. Most tags come in pairs and surround text. Tags are identified by angle brackets <>. Tags contain instructions that explain to browsers what they should do or how they should display the text they surround. The beginning tag turns the tag "on," and the ending tag, along with the slash (/) mark, turns the tag "off."

Hint: Test nested tags using different graphical browsers to make sure they actually produce the visual effect you expect to see. Test them also using a text-only browser; sometimes nesting tags can create unusually formatted text.

<TAG>text**</TAG>**
<STRONG>Oh boy!**</STRONG>**

A few tags are *single tags* because they contain no text, but only instruct browsers to display something or format a document in a particular way. Single tags are also referred to as *empty tags*. Typical single tags are the <BR> tag, which breaks a line of text and starts text on the following line, and the <HR> tag, which draws a line across a page.

Tag text is case-insensitive and can be written in either upper, lower, or mixed case.

<html> <HTML> <HtMl>

You can combine (or nest) tags inside other tags for a combined effect.

<B><I>Internet Tutorials for Teens**</I></B>**

ATTRIBUTES

Attributes are variables that can be used, or not used, with tags. Attributes define special conditions or give special instruction about how a tag will be used, displayed, or be placed in a Web document. Attributes are always included inside the beginning tag. Attribute text, like tag text, is case-insensitive.

<IMG SRC=> <img src=> <IMG src=> <Img Src=>

The values associated with attributes may be case-sensitive. If you put an attribute in quotation marks, the value must be expressed exactly as it is inside the quotation marks. If you don't put the value in quotation marks, then the value can be expressed in upper, lower, or mixed case.

<IMG SRC="OPLIN.gif">

The name of the file must be typed in uppercase, the file extension in lowercase.

<TH ALIGN=left> <TH ALIGN=LEFT>

A standard HTML value for the ALIGN= attribute.

HTML DOCUMENT FORMATTING

HTML ignores extra spaces and blank lines in documents. It also ignores keyboard commands like returns and tabs as well as the characters you produce by holding down the CTRL or ALT keys in combination with keyboard keys. To simulate tabs, indents, or other formatting commands you must use specific HTML tags that produce similar results.

There is no one standard way to use tags within a document. Some people prefer to write HTML documents so that there is only one tag or tag group per line; others write HTML documents as long continuous paragraphs of text and tags. Most people fall in between these two extremes. Choose an HTML formatting style for your Web site, create an HTML template, and have everyone who adds to, or changes, your Web pages use the same tagging style. If you don't, it might be difficult to quickly update your Web site.

SPECIAL CHARACTER EQUIVALENTS

HTML can display characters commonly found on computer keyboards and a whole bunch of other characters not found on many computer, or even typewriter keyboards (e.g., foreign diacritical marks, the copyright symbol, the British Pound sign, inverted question, and exclamation marks). In order to get these to display on Web pages, you'll need to use the special character equivalents listed in Appendix C.

There are two different ways to express character equivalents, either as a number or as an abbreviated name (which *is* case-sensitive). In either case, all equivalents start with an ampersand (**&**) and end with a semicolon (**;**).

resumé
resumé

Both create the word "resume" with an acute mark over the "e."

Three other characters that show up on your computer keyboard also have special character equivalents. These are the characters (angle brackets (<>), quotation marks ("), ampersands (&)), which are used in HTML tagging. If you need to use one of these characters, you'll need to use its equivalent character. Otherwise, your browser will not be able to tell a bracketed word from an HTML tag, a hypertext link URL in quotation marks from a quoted piece of text, or the start of an equivalent character from a regular ampersand.

Welcome to the **"**Just for Kids**"** storytime area
Welcome to the **"**Just for Kids**"** storytime area
Tags look like this—**<**TITLE**>**
Baker **&** Taylor

WEB SITE ORGANIZATION AND DESIGN

Creating a Power Web Site focuses on the technical aspects of upgrading your Web site rather than on the organizational and design issues that you must also consider. For thorough coverage of the planning steps for creating or upgrading your library Web site, as well as library-specific information about Web site organization, design, and technological considerations, read *Using the World Wide Web and Creating Home Pages*, by Ray E. Metz and Gail Junion-Metz (one of Neal-Schuman's "How-To" books).

We've also included citations to many good books on general Web site design and creating Web graphics in Appendix B.

2

HTML Tags

*An HTML file containing most of the tagging samples from this chapter can be found in the HTML folder on the CD-ROM under: **2.html**.*

INTRODUCTION

This chapter will help familiarize you with the HTML tags you will be using to "power up" your Web site. The tags described in this chapter come from both HTML 2 and various HTML 3 versions. This chapter describes most, but not all, HTML tags (including some of the Netscape and Internet Explorer specific tags and attributes that will be identified as such). The major tags and attributes you will use most are described in this chapter (except for those associated with style sheets). Most of the more esoteric, specialized, little-used, or unused tags and attributes have been left out. For a full description of all HTML tags and attributes, consult one of the HTML texts listed in Appendix B.

For the most part, tag and attribute descriptions have been kept brief. We've included examples to help you understand how different tags and attributes function. Fuller descriptions, more examples, and directions for using various tags to build tables, frames, imagemaps, and forms are described in Chapters 4–9.

In order to help you better understand differing tags that have similar functions, we have organized HTML tags into the following sub-groupings:

- tags that identify and name documents
- tags that organize Web page contents
- an important tag that doesn't show
- tags that separate text
- tags that affect how text displays
- other text tags

- tags that create different types of lists
- tags that affect how graphics display
- tags that create hypertext links
- tags that create imagemaps
- tags that create tables
- tags that create frames
- tags that create forms

TAGS THAT IDENTIFY AND NAME DOCUMENTS

Starting and ending tags help browsers display your Web pages correctly. These tags do not affect the line-by-line appearance of your documents, but give browsers instructions about the nature and length of each document and how different pages are labeled.

HTML TAG <HTML>

The first and last tag of every HTML document is the <HTML> </HTML> tag pair. These tags specify when an HTML document starts and when it stops.

```
<HTML>
your document
</HTML>
```

Attributes You Can Use with the <HTML> Tag

VERSION= The VERSION= attribute allows you to let users know what version of HTML you used to create the document.

```
VERSION="HTML3.0"
```

HEAD TAG <HEAD>

The <HEAD> </HEAD> tag pair is usually the second tag of every document. The <HEAD> always must contain a <TITLE> tag and can optionally contain other tags, which will be covered later in this chapter.

```
<HTML>
<HEAD>
<TITLE> Overman College Library</TITLE>
</HEAD>
your document
</HTML>
```

3 1833 03634 7901

TITLE TAG <TITLE>

The <TITLE> </TITLE> tag pair is found inside the <HEAD> tags. It identifies the title of the document, which, depending on the browser, will be displayed in the window bar or indented at the start of the home page text. The text you put in the title tag also can describe the document when you save it as a bookmark. There can only be one title per HTML document and it can only contain text (no links).

> **Hint:** Many browsers limit the number of letters/ numbers that display for the title, so it is best to keep titles short, 30–40 characters.

> **<TITLE>** Overman College Library**</TITLE>**
> **<TITLE>** Honor Public Library**</TITLE>**
> **<TITLE>** Washington HS Library**</TITLE>**

TAGS THAT ORGANIZE WEB PAGE CONTENTS

Structure tags help create the basic look of a Web page. You use them to create headlines and to break up information into meaningful pieces. List tags are also structure tags, but because there are so many ways to create lists, we describe them in a separate section.

BODY TAG <BODY>

Inside the <BODY> </BODY> tag pair you'll find the text and tags that make up the majority of an HTML document. All the text inside these tags will be visible to patrons looking at your HTML document using a browser. Those tags before or after the body tag will not be visible, except when patrons look at the document's HTML source coding. The <BODY> tag can contain various attributes that affect how patrons will see your Web page.

> **<HTML>**
> **<HEAD>**
> **<TITLE>** Skillen College Library**</TITLE>**
> **</HEAD>**
> **<BODY BACKGROUND=**"white-mi.jpg" **LINK="CC3300">**
> what patrons see when connecting to your Webpage
> **</BODY>**
> **</HTML>**

Attributes You Can Use with the <BODY> Tag

ALINK= The ALINK= identifies an active link and is the attribute that specifies a hexadecimal color that the link will turn when it is selected.

> **ALINK="FF3399"**

Will create a hot pink link when clicked.

BACKGROUND= The BACKGROUND= attribute contains a graphic file name that is used for the background of your Web page. These graphics can be either in .GIF or .JPEG formats. The image files themselves are quite small, but are put together, like pieces of wallpaper, to create a composite image.

BGCOLOR= The BGCOLOR= attribute contains the hexadecimal color that will be used for the Web page's background color. (See Appendix C for a listing of all hexadecimal color codes.)

BGCOLOR="004400"

LINK= The LINK= attribute contains the hexadecimal color code that will be used for the Web page's unvisited links.

TEXT= The TEXT= attribute contains the hexadecimal color code that will be used for the Web page's text.

Hint: The generic VLINK color is purple, now you can make it orange if you wish.

VLINK= The VLINK= attribute contains the hexadecimal color code that will be used for links you've already visited.

HEADER TAGS <H1> . . . <H6>

Header tag pairs <H1> </H1> structure your document like an outline. It is best to use header tags in descending numerical order starting with <H1> and ending with <H6> .

Hint: There are fourth, fifth, and sixth level header tags <H4> <H5> <H6>. These are normally not used unless the Web page structure is solely in outline form or very complex.

First level header tags <H1> are like the major section heads in an outline. (<H1> tags are often used as the main "headlines" for individual Web pages.) Second level header tags <H2> are like the second level of headings in an outline. (They often are used to subdivide major parts of Web pages.) Third level header tags <H3> often indicate important sub-categories under major text groupings.

There is no limit to the number, words, etc., you can use as header text. Like newspaper headlines or outline text, use common sense and keep text short and to the point. Each header tag displays differently (e.g., bold and indented, bold not indented). You can include either plain text and/or hypertext links in headers. Each browser displays the various levels of headers slightly differently, so it's important to check how each type of header displays.

Attributes You Can Use with <H> Tags

ALIGN= The ALIGN= attribute allows you to align the header line three ways: LEFT, RIGHT or CENTER.

ALIGN="CENTER"

Will center header text on the screen.

CLEAR= The CLEAR= attribute specifies where the next line of text after the header starts. There are three values for the CLEAR= attribute, RIGHT that moves the text downward until the right margin is clear. LEFT that moves the text downward until the text can be placed along the left margin, and ALL that moves the text down until both margins are clear.

NOWRAP The NOWRAP attribute specifies that the header should not word wrap automatically. Use the <BR> tag to specify where you want a browser to break the header.

> **<H1>** Overman College Library**</H1>**
> **<H2>** Virtual Reference Desk**</H2>**
> **<H3>** Business Resources**</H3>**

META TAG <META>

The single <META> tag is placed inside of the <HEAD> tag. It provides a place to put information that doesn't fit into the other tags.

Attributes You Can Use with <META> Tags

NAME= The NAME= attribute contains a name for the information found in the CONTENT= attribute. If you are adding keywords, the NAME= attribute often is called "keywords"

CONTENT= If you use either the NAME= or HTTP-EQUIV= attribute, you must first use the CONTENT= attribute. The CONTENT= attribute contains the information referenced from the other two attributes. If you are listing keywords, you put them into the CONTENT= attribute.

HTTP-EQUIV= This attribute allows you to send appropriate HTTP response headers back to the server delivering the document. If you want to use this attribute, consult a detailed HTML reference source.

BASE URL TAG <BASE>

The single <BASE> tag is placed within the <HEAD> tag and indicates the URL where the document is located. The URL in the tag can be the one where it is now located or where it was originally located and now no longer resides. If you don't include this tag, most browsers will default to the URL used to access the Web site. Some browsers bookmark the base URL and others the typed URL.

Attributes You Can Use with <BASE> Tags

HREF= The HREF= attribute specifies the URL you wish to use as the base URL.

TARGET= The TARGET= attribute specifies the name of the file that can open a separate window display. Since browsers can open multiple Web windows, setting up a targeted link can open up a separate window for the link, while keeping the original win-

Hint: Different browsers and different computers (PC and Mac) handle text and pictures very differently. You will want to experiment with the CLEAR= attribute to see which value works best for your Web site.

Hint: Use the <META> tag to store keywords related to your Web page. When search engines visit your Web site, they'll find words to index your site by, other than the words you use in the document itself.

dow and links open in the background, or you can use the TARGET= attribute to open a specific frame in a framed display.

<BASE HREF="http://www.oplin.lib.oh.us/"**>**
<BASE TARGET="frame2"**>**

LINK TAG <LINK>

The single <LINK> tag describes the relationship between the document you have created and another HTML document. Often you will use this tag to point to previous or next documents. Link tags are constructed very much like Anchor <A> tags. When in doubt whether you should use <LINK> or <A> , use <A>.

Attributes You Can Use with <LINK> Tags

HREF= The HREF= attribute specifies the file name or URL of the related document.

HREF=file2.html

The document is named file1.html

REL= The REL= attribute specifies the relationship between the document and another document in the Web site. Some of the relationships that can be named are HOME, NEXT, PREVIOUS, TOC, UP, and HELP.

REV= The REV= attribute is similar to the REL= attribute but the relationship is from a related document back to the base/original document.

TITLE= The TITLE= attribute allows users to preview the title of the document that is hypertext linked prior to actually connecting to and loading the document.

BACKGROUND SOUND TAG <BGSOUND>

The single <BGSOUND> tag (Microsoft only) is most often found inside the <BODY> tag. It specifies an inline audio file that will play once the Web page is loaded.

Attributes You Can Use with <BGSOUND> Tags

LOOP= The LOOP= attribute specifies how many times the audio file will play before stopping.

LOOP=10

Means that the audio file will repeat itself 10 times and then quit.

SRC= The SRC= attribute specifies the audio file name that you want to play when the page is loaded.

EMBED TAG <EMBED>

Similar to the <BGSOUND> tag, this tag (Netscape only) creates a little player console window that pops onto the screen when a sound file is selected.

Attributes You Can Use with <EMBED> Tags

AUTOSTART= The AUTOSTART= attribute has two values, TRUE and FALSE. If you set the value to TRUE the sound file will play automatically when the console box appears on the screen. If set to FALSE a visitor has to select the play button on the console.

CONTROLS= The CONTROLS= attribute has two values, CONSOLE and SMALLCONSOLE. Choose a large or small player console by choosing either value.

LOOP= The LOOP= attribute specifies the number of times the sound file will play before it stops.

SRC= The SRC= attribute specifies the URL of the sound file that will play.

VOLUME= The volume attribute presets the volume of the sound file that will play. The value can be between 1 and 255.

Hint: Volume=255 is *very* loud, so experiment with the volume to make sure the sound file is not too loud or soft.

AN IMPORTANT TAG THAT DOESN'T SHOW . . .

Comments Tag <!— —>

This odd looking single tag <!— —> is important because browsers don't display the text included inside it. The comments tag displays in your HTML document and contains internal comments that you only want your staff to see. You can use this tag to ask fellow HTML team members to check your tagging or to include information about who added or revised a link or to indicate the source of information. You can also add keywords in comments tags so that Web search engines can find them when they index your Web site. You can compose comments using upper and lower case letters, or just upper case letters, so they stand out in your HTML document. (This is one case where all caps doesn't translate into screaming your message, like it does in e-mail or Usenet newsgroups.) There is no limit to the length or content of comment tags, so be creative when using them.

<!—Please check this tagged section for accuracy—>
<!—Link suggested by George B. 6/5/97—>
<!—URL REVISED ON 2/10/98—>

TAGS THAT SEPARATE TEXT

PARAGRAPH TAG <P>

The single paragraph tag <P> places a space between lines or blocks of text. If you use more than one <P> tag to create multiple lines of space, you may find that some browsers will ignore all but the first <P> tag and only create one space for you.

<P>
This is text
<P>
This is more text

Attributes You Can Use with <P> Tags

ALIGN= The ALIGN= attribute allows you to align text four ways: LEFT, RIGHT, or CENTER and JUSTIFY

ALIGN="LEFT"

Will align text that follows the tag along the left margin.

NOWRAP The NOWRAP attribute specifies that text will not word wrap. Use the <BR> tag to indicate where text should be broken and begin a new line of text.

HORIZONTAL RULE TAG <HR>

This single tag <HR> does not contain any text. It simply creates a shaded line that can be used:

1. To separate headlines from body text.
2. To separate major sections within the body text.
3. To separate body text from navigation buttons and Web page information at the bottom of a page. Like any graphical element, use it sparingly and consistently for the greatest impact.

Attributes You Can Use with <HR> Tags

ALIGN= The ALIGN= attribute allows you to align the line created by the <HR> tag three ways: LEFT, RIGHT, or CENTER

ALIGN="CENTER"

Will center the line on the page.

NOSHADE The NOSHADE attribute creates a solid black line, rather than the default shaded line.

SIZE= The SIZE= attribute specifies how thick the line will be (expressed in pixels)

SIZE=5

Means that the line will be 5 pixels wide.

WIDTH= The WIDTH= attribute specifies the width of line. The size of the line is expressed either in pixels or in a percentage of the page

WIDTH=75% or WIDTH=80

Means that the line will be only the designated size related to the document.

COLOR= This COLOR= attribute is used with the Internet Explorer browser. This attribute specifies the color of the line using hexadecimal color codes.

COLOR="CC0000"

Will mean the text will be bright red.

TEXT BREAK TAG

This single tag <BR> is used to stop text and restart again on the next line. It's similar to a hard return in a wordprocessing environment. The <BR> tag is placed at the end of each line of text.

Roses are red**
**
Violets are blue**
**
I think HTML is easy**
**
And so will you**
**

Attributes You Can Use with
 Tags

CLEAR= The CLEAR= attribute allows you to specify where the next line starts. This is especially important when using a <BR> so that text flows correctly around a graphic. There are three values for the CLEAR= attribute, RIGHT that moves text downward until the right margin is clear, LEFT that moves text downward until the text can be placed along the left margin, and ALL that moves text down until both margins are clear.

NOBREAK TAG <NOBR>

The <NOBR> </NOBR> tag pair specifies that text should not be influenced by line breaks or word wrapping. Text inside <NOBR> tags will be displayed as a single line of text. If the line is long enough it will scroll off the page, in which case you'll see a horizontal scroll bar appear at the bottom of your browser screen.

Hint: Different browsers and different platforms (PC and Mac) handle text and graphics very differently. Be sure to experiment with the CLEAR− attribute to see which works best for your Web site.

WORD BREAK TAG <WBR>

The single <WBR> is used within the <NOBR> tag pair. The <WBR> tag specifies where a word break is allowed. Use this tag, instead of the standard <BR> tag to stop text and start a new line.

DIVISION OF TEXT <DIV>

Hint: Use <DIV> for references to other works, long quotes, or just for giving a section of text graphic significance.

The <DIV> </DIV> tag pair marks a block of text so that you can set up specific characteristics for that block.

Attributes You Can Use with <DIV> Tags

ALIGN= The ALIGN= attribute allows you to align blocks of text three ways: LEFT, RIGHT, or CENTER

ALIGN="CENTER"

Will center the block of text.

Hint: Browsers and computers handle this attribute differently. Be sure to experiment with the CLEAR= attribute to see which works best for your Web site.

CLEAR= The CLEAR= attribute specifies where the next line of text starts. There are three values for the CLEAR= attribute, RIGHT that moves text downward until the right margin is clear, LEFT that moves text downward until the text can be placed along the left margin, and ALL that moves text down until both margins are clear.

NOWRAP The NOWRAP attribute specifies not to word wrap the text automatically, but to look for <BR> tags, which specifically indicate text breaks and where a new line begins.

TAGS THAT AFFECT HOW TEXT DISPLAYS

Text tags affect the graphical look of the text itself. There are two types of tags: logical tags and physical tags. *Logical tags* indicate how the text is used but do not dictate how browsers must display them. *Physical tags*, on the other hand, tell browsers precisely how you want the text displayed (e.g., italics). Of the two types, logical tags are more flexible because they let browsers decide how to display the text in the manner appropriate for that browser. As a result, HTML documents with logical tags have a better chance of displaying well with a variety of browser software.

PHYSICAL STYLES

BOLD TEXT <B>

The <B> </B> tag pair tells browsers to display the text as bold.

Intellectual freedom is **<B>**very**</B>** important

BIG TEXT <BIG>

The <BIG> </BIG> tag pair tells browsers to display the text slightly bigger than the surrounding text.

There is a **<BIG>** self-check machine**</BIG>** near the front door

ITALIC TEXT <I>

The <I> </I> tag pair tells browsers to display the text as italics.

<I>When**</I>** is the library open?

SMALL TEXT <SMALL>

The <SMALL> </SMALL> tag pair tells browsers to display text slightly smaller than the surrounding text.

Check out **<SMALL>** tiny**</SMALL>** books this week

STRIKE THROUGH TEXT <STRIKE>

This <STRIKE> </STRIKE> tag pair tells browser to display text with a line though it.

<STRIKE>Bibliographic Instruction**</STRIKE>** should be replaced by the phrase Library Instruction.

SUBSCRIPT TEXT <SUB>

The tag pair tells browsers to display text slightly below other text.

The chemical formula for water is H**_{**2**}**0

> **Hint:** Be careful using italicized text. On monitors set to a low-resolution display, italicized text appears fuzzy and can be difficult to read.

> **Hint:** Use <STRIKE> for showing changes from an old version of a document to a newer version.

SUPERSCRIPT TEXT <SUP>

Hint: Use <SUP>
for footnote
references.

The tag pair tells browser to display text slightly above other text.

   The chemical formula for carbon dioxide is CO**²**

TYPED TEXT TAG <TT>

The <TT> </TT> tag pair tells browsers to display the text a fixed-width font such as Courier.

   To exit the program, type **<TT>quit</TT>**

UNDERLINED TEXT <U>

The <U> </U> tag pair tells browsers to display the text with underlining.

   Hypertext links display like **<U>this</U>** on the screen

LOGICAL STYLES

ABBREVIATION <ABBREV>

The <ABBREV> </ABBREV> tag pair identifies the text as an abbreviation.

ACRONYM <ACRONYM>

The <ACRONYM> </ACRONYM> tag pair identifies the text as an acronym.

AUTHOR NAME <AU>

The <AU> </AU> tag pair identifies the text as one, or several, author names.

BASEFONT <BASEFONT>

This single tag identifies the size of the font for the whole HTML document.

Attributes That Are Used with the <BASEFONT> Tag

SIZE= The SIZE= attribute contains the font size expressed as a number.

   SIZE=12

Will mean that the font used in the whole HTML document will display in 12-point letters.

BLINKING TEXT <BLINK>

The <BLINK> </BLINK> tag pair (Netscape only) identifies text that will blink when displayed on a browser screen.

> Bring your books back by **<BLINK>**June 17th**</BLINK>**

Hint: Please use <BLINK> sparingly! Most people find blinking text very annoying.

CITED TEXT <CITE>

This tag pair <CITE> </CITE> identifies text as a citation.

> **<CITE>**A. Lipow, 1997.**</CITE>**

DEFINED TEXT <DFN>

This tag pair <DFN> </DFN> identifies text that is being defined. Most graphical browsers display <DFN> tagged text in bold.

> **<DFN>**Virus**</DFN>** is short for computer virus

DELETED TEXT <DEL>

The <DEL> </DEL> tag pair (Netscape only) identifies text that has been deleted. You can also use the <STRIKE> tag to achieve similar results.

Hint: Use <DEL> when showing revised versions of procedures or policies.

EMPHASIZED TEXT <EM>

The <EM> </EM> tag pair identifies text that should be emphasized. Most graphical browsers display <EM> tagged text in italics.

> Intellectual freedom is **<EM>**very**</EM>** important

FONT SIZE <FONT>

The <FONT> tag identifies the size of type to display on a Web page, using a numerical scale from 1 to 7 (seven being the largest and one the smallest.)

Attributes You Can Use with the <FONT> Tag

COLOR= The COLOR= attribute specifies a hexadecimal color for the text.

> **COLOR="CC3300"**

Will produce dark orange text.

Hint: Be sure to choose a commonly used font when applying the FACE= attribute to make sure the results on a visitor's screen matches your coding. If a specified font is not available on a visitor's computer, the browser will ignore this attribute and default to its own base font. You can also specify multiple fonts, so that if the first is not applicable, it will default to the second or third font.

FACE= The FACE= attribute specifies the font to use when displaying the page.

FACE="Comic Sans MS"

Will mean that your Web page displays the Comic Sans font when viewed by visitors.

SIZE= This attribute specifies the size of the font in numbers 1 to 7.

INSERTED TEXT <INS>

The <INS> </INS> identifies the text (Netscape only) as newly inserted in the document.

KEYBOARDED TEXT <KBD>

The <KBD> </KBD> tag pair identifies the text that a patron would either see on a computer screen, or type using a computer keyboard. Most graphical browsers display <KBD> tagged text as a fixed-width, mono-spaced font such as Courier.

<KBD>telnet</KBD>

Hint: Use <INS> to show changes between old and new procedures and policies.

QUOTED TEXT <Q>

The <Q> </Q> tag pair (Netscape only) identifies text as a short quotation. Text within these tags will be automatically surrounded with quotation marks. (For longer quotes, use the <BLOCKQUOTE> tag pair.)

He said **<Q>**Librarians will be leaders in the digital age **</Q>** in 1992

SAMPLE TEXT <SAMP>

The <SAMP> </SAMP> tag pair identifies text as sample characters. This tag is usually printed in a fixed-width font like Courier.

To register on-line, type **<SAMP>**your name**</SAMP>** in the box below

STRONG TEXT <STRONG>

The <STRONG> </STRONG> tag pair identifies text that should be strongly emphasized. Most graphical browsers display <STRONG> tagged text in bold.

Intellectual freedom is **<STRONG>**very**</STRONG>**important

VARIABLE TEXT <VAR>

The tag pair <VAR> </VAR> identifies information that a patron would type on a computer keyboard. Most graphical browsers treat <VAR> tagged text in either italics or as underlined.

<KBD>telnet**</KBD><VAR>**Internet address of remote computer **</VAR>**

OTHER TEXT TAGS

ADDRESS TEXT <ADDRESS>

The <ADDRESS> </ADDRESS> tag pair is often found at the bottom of each page. It contains information about the Web page author or library and often a copyright statement, e-mail address of the Webmaster, and a date when the page was last revised. Address information displays differently on various browsers.

<ADDRESS>
Honor Public Library**
**
copyright 1998**
**
revised 2/21/98**
**
</ADDRESS>

Hint: One browser may italicize ADDRESS text, another indent it, and still another may right justify it. so be sure to test this tag thoroughly.

BLOCK QUOTATION TAG <BLOCKQUOTE>

The <BLOCKQUOTE> </BLOCKQUOTE> tag pair specifies a block of text as a quotation. Each browser handles this tag slightly differently. Most indent text within the tags and most create additional white space both before and after the text.

<BLOCKQUOTE>
<P>
"Four score and twenty years ago . . . "
<P>
</BLOCKQUOTE>

Hint: The odd thing about this tag is that you cannot place text directly inside it. Text must be within list <LI> or paragraph <P> tags.

CENTERED TEXT <CENTER>

The <CENTER> </CENTER> tag pair will center text on your computer screen.

<CENTER>
2418 K Street**
**
Honor, OH 44230**
**
330–555–1234**
**
</CENTER>

Hint: For best graphic effect, use this tag sparingly.

TYPED CODE <CODE>

Hint: Use
<CODE> to display
single lines or
short sections of
programming code
like PERL.

The <CODE> </CODE> tag pair specifies that text should displayed in a fixed-width font like Courier and that it should have white space around it to set it apart from the rest of the text.

   <CODE>$user=$in{'user'};**</CODE>**

PREFORMATTED TEXT <PRE>

The <PRE> </PRE> tag pair takes whatever text you put inside them and formats it on the screen exactly as you did, leaving the white space and text to display as you typed it. One way you can use <PRE> tags is to take pre-existing text and tag it quickly for inclusion on your Web site. You can also use <PRE> tags to create columns of information, or to create multiple lines of white space between lines/blocks of text. Preformatted text has one less-than-optimal feature: it displays text in a mono-spaced font such as Courier.

Hint: Keep lines to
80 characters or
less.

Hint: If you use too
much pre-
formatted text on
your Web pages it
can look quite
amateurish, so use
it sparingly and
only when
necessary.

   <PRE>$6,500.00 for books $ 4,725.00 for media
        $8,000.00 for hardware $12,000.00 for software**</PRE>**

   <PRE>March 9th is our annual Friends of the Library Book Sale!**</PRE>**

   first, let's visit Dogpile
   <PRE>

   </PRE>
   next, let's visit MetaCrawler

Attributes You Can Use with <PRE> Tags

Hint: Use the
WIDTH feature so
that text within
<PRE> tags does
not extend beyond
the edge of the
screen, so that
patrons need not
use the horizontal
scroll bar. Some
browser versions
ignore this
attribute, so be
sure to test it
locally to see that
it works.

WIDTH= The WIDTH= attribute specifies the maximum number of characters to display on a single line. After that browsers are free to word wrap.

TAGS THAT CREATE DIFFERENT TYPES OF LISTS

LIST TAG <LI>

The single <LI> tag identifies a single element in most lists.

Attributes You Can Use with <LI> Tags

TYPE= Depending on whether the <LI> tag is part of an ordered or unordered list, the value of the TYPE= attribute will change. In an ordered list, the attribute allows you to specify which type of ordering elements you want: upper-/lowercase letters, upper-/lowercase roman numerals, or standard numbering. Set the value to a or A for upper- and lowercase letters, i or I for upper- or lowercase roman numerals, and 1 for regular numbering. In an unordered list, the attribute allows you to specify which type of symbol to display before list elements: a filled-in circle, an open circle, or a square. Set the value to DISC for a filled-in circle symbol, CIRCLE for an open circle symbol or SQUARE a square bullet.

VALUE= The VALUE= attribute allows you to specify which number you wish a list item to have.

VALUE=6.

List items would increment starting from 6.

DIRECTORY LIST TAG <DIR>

Use the directory list tag pair <DIR> </DIR> when you have a list that contains short descriptive elements, less than 25 characters per description. The <LI> tag identifies each list element. Most browsers place some sort of symbol/bullet before each list element. This will vary from browser to browser. Some browsers will also indent list elements, others will not.

Attributes You Can Use with <DIR> Tags

COMPACT The COMPACT attribute specifies that the list should display with less white space between text elements. This can be helpful if you want a visitor to see a whole list without having to use a scroll bar. Not all versions of browsers recognize the COMPACT attribute. Check to be sure that the browser version you use supports it.

*For examples of the different list types, see the file **2.html** in the HTML folder on the CD-ROM.*

Hint: If list elements are short, it may display in multiple columns. Therefore, be sure to test <DIR> lists using different browsers, browser versions, and different computers.

MENU LIST TAG <MENU>

The tag pair <MENU> </MENU> is used for short lists of briefly described items . . . even shorter than a directory list. The <LI> tag identifies each list element. Menu lists are usually displayed in a more compact manner than directory lists. Often browsers treat menu lists just like bulleted <UL> lists.

Attributes You Can Use with <MENU> Tags

COMPACT The COMPACT attribute specifies that the list should display with less white space between text elements.

ORDERED LIST TAG <OL>

Use the <OL> </OL> tag pair to set up an ordered list. This type of list is also called a *numbered list*. Rather than numbering each item in the list, an ordered list identifies each list element displaying the <LI> tag and leaves it to your browser to number them correctly.

> **Hint:** When you add or delete something from an ordered list, the numbering is always correct.

Attributes You Can Use with <OL> Tags

COMPACT The COMPACT attribute specifies that the list should display with less white space between text elements.

START= The START= attribute specifies which number you wish the list to start with.

> **START=10**

Will start the list with number 10 and increment upwards.

TYPE= The TYPE= attribute specifies which type of ordering elements you want: upper-/lowercase letters, upper-/lowercase roman numerals, or standard numbering. Set the value to a or A for upper- or lowercase letters, i or I for upper or lowercase roman numerals, and 1 for regular numbering.

UNORDERED LIST TAG <UL>

Use the <UL> </UL> tag pair to set up an unordered list. This type of list is also called a *bulleted list*. Each item in an ordered list is preceded by a bullet rather than a number or letter. The <LI> tag specifies that text is part of the list. How the bullet looks depends on the browser patrons are using.

Attributes You Can Use with <UL> Tags

COMPACT The COMPACT attribute specifies that the list should display with less white space between text elements.

TYPE= The TYPE= attribute specifies which type of symbol you want it to display before list elements: a filled-in circle, an open circle, or a square. Set the value to DISC for a filled-in circle symbol, CIRCLE for an open circle symbol or SQUARE a square bullet.

TYPE="DISC"

GLOSSARY LIST TAG <DL>

The <DL> </DL> tag pair appears at the beginning and end of a glossary list, also called a *definition list*. A glossary list is one of the few list types that allows you to create an indented, outline-like appearance. The <DL> tag is used in combination with the <DT> and <DD> tags to create a glossary list.

Attributes You Can Use with <DL> Tags

COMPACT The COMPACT attribute specifies that the list should display with less white space between text elements.

DEFINED TERM TAG <DT>

The <DT> tag is used along with the <DL> and <DD> tags. The <DL> tag defines a term in a glossary list that you wish to have left justified. Most people use just a single <DT> tag, but you can use the optional </DT> tag if you wish. There are no attributes for the <DT> tag.

DEFINITION TAG <DD>

The <DD> tag is always used in combination with the <DT> tag. It identifies the text that should be indented beneath <DT> tagged text. Most people use just a single <DD> tag, but you can use the optional </DD> tag if you wish. There are no attributes for the <DD> tag.

LIST EXAMPLES

MENU AND DIRECTORY LISTS

Library Procedure Manual
<MENU>
<LI>Circulation
<LI>Interlibrary loan
<LI>Reference
<LI>Periodicals
</MENU>

> **Hint:** <TYPE> does not match SGML syntax; use it only when sure that it will work for the majority of your patrons.

York Library Services
<DIR>
<LI>Hours we're open
<LI>24 hour reference
<LI>Story hour for kids
<LI>Seniors outreach
<LI>Cyberlibrary
</DIR>

NUMBERED (ORDERED) LIST

Getting a Book from InterLibrary Loan
<OL>
<LI>Bring us the author, title, publisher of each book you want
<LI>Fill out an ILL form for each book
<LI>Bring to ILL 9–5 Mon. - Fri.
<LI>Pick up your material after you receive notification
</OL>

BULLETED (UNORDERED) LIST

Internet Tutorials for Teens
<UL>
<LI>What's the Web and why should I care?
<LI>What's a browser and how do they work?
<LI>Netscape power-tips . . . become a super user!
<LI>Different cool search tools
<LI>Searching power tips . . . become a super searcher!
<LI>Once you've found it, then what?!
<LI>Printing, downloading Web stuff
<LI>Being cool (and safe) while on-line
</UL>

GLOSSARY (DEFINITION) LIST

Honor Library
<DL>
<DT>Services
    <DD>Circulation
    <DD>Reference
    <DD>InterLibrary Loan
<DT>Collections
    <DD>Books
    <DD>Periodicals / Microforms
    <DD>Multimedia / Audio-visual
</DL>

COMBINED LISTS

It is possible to combine list types to create a variety of visual effects.

Hint: Browsers display each type of list differently. When combining different lists check to see that they create the visual effect you want.

> Getting a Book from Inter-Library Loan
> **<OL>**
> **<LI>**Check our catalog first to make sure we don't already have the book
> **<LI>**Fill out an ILL form for each book you want us to get
>   **<UL>**
>   **<LI>**Include as much of the author's name and title as you know
>   **<LI>**Include as much publication information (publisher, date, edition) as you know
>   **<LI>**Fill out your name, address, phone, email so we can contact you
>   **</UL>**
> **<LI>**Drop off the forms at the ILL office 9–5 Mon.—Fri.
> **<LI>**Stop in 3 days after you receive notification that we have your book(s)
> **</OL>**

Note: We use indentions to make it easier for you to see the structure of this type of list. Web browsers ignore tabs and indents, so using indentions makes reviewing and revising Web pages much simpler.

TAGS THAT AFFECT HOW GRAPHICS DISPLAY

IMAGE TAG <IMG>

The single <IMG> tag identifies an inline graphic that will automatically load along with Web page text.

Attributes You Can Use with the <IMG> Tag

SRC= *Mandatory* The SRC= attribute lists the local file name or URL of the image to be loaded.

ALIGN= There are lots of options for aligning graphics. The first two options place graphics horizontally on a page. LEFT places the image near the left margin and RIGHT places the image near the right margin. The next options place graphics in relation to surrounding text. The TOP option places the top of the graphic in line with text. The MIDDLE option centers the graphic vertically with the text, and the BOTTOM option aligns the bottom of the graphic with the text.

ALT= The ALT= attribute provides a text description of the image for those with slow modems or text-only browsers. Text should be placed in square brackets.

Hint: If you don't want any description for a purely decorative image, use ALT= " "

> **ALT= [Animated book]**

BORDER= The BORDER= attribute specifies a specific width border around an image, when that image is also a hypertext link. The value is expressed in pixels.

BORDER=3

Means that the link border around the graphic will be 3 pixels wide.

HEIGHT= The HEIGHT= attribute specifies the height of the image. It is expressed in pixels.

Hint: HEIGHT= can help you quickly resize images so they are the right size for your Web page.

HEIGHT=35

Means the image displayed will be 35 pixels high, even if the original image was a different size.

HSPACE= The HSPACE= attribute creates white space between an image and the text that is next to it.

Hint: HSPACE can make your Web page graphics stand out more by creating white space between text and the start of the graphic.

HSPACE=5

Will create 5 pixels of white space between the picture and the text.

ISMAP The ISMAP attribute specifies the image is "active" and is part of an imagemap.

LOWSRC= The LOWSRC= attribute (Netscape only) specifies the URL of a small- or low-resolution, or black-and-white image, that will load before the larger, high resolution color image.

Hint: LOWSRC is a nifty feature when patrons have slow modems or the image is large and takes quite a while to load. . . . like an imagemap graphic.

USEMAP= The USEMAP= attribute specifies the name of the active image or image map that a graphic represents.

VSPACE= The VSPACE= attribute creates white space vertically between an image and the text that is above or below it.

Hint: VPSACE= can make your Web page graphics stand out from text that surrounds it.

VSPACE=10

Will create 10 pixels of white space between the picture and the text.

WIDTH= The WIDTH= attribute specifies the width of a displayed graphic. It is expressed in pixels.

Hint: WIDTH= can help you quickly resize graphics so they are the right size for your Web page.

WIDTH=20

Means the image displayed will be 20 pixels wide, even if the original image was a different size.

TAGS THAT CREATE HYPERTEXT LINKS

Creating hypertext/hypermedia links in Web documents—so that patrons can access different parts of your Web site or Web pages located on computers around the world—is just as important as tagging document text so that it is easy to read and interpret.

Links consist of three elements: HTML tags and attributes; information you want to link to, expressed as file names or URLs; and words or graphics that act as links to URLs or file names.

You can create different types of links. Links to information on your Web server are called *internal links*. Links to information out there on the Internet are called *external links*. Links can be represented by words, pictures, or both.

In order to make creating links to HTML documents and URLs to Internet tools as simple as possible, we provide you with step-by-step directions for creating basic internal and external links, as well as examples of basic links to media.

ANCHOR TAG <A>

Anchor tags <A></A> specifies text that should be treated as a link. Information inside of anchor tags identify the location of the information and how the link will be displayed on your Web page.

Attributes You Can Use with <A> Tags

HREF= The HREF= attribute specifies the file name or URL that you wish to make a hypertext link. Either the HREF= or NAME= attributes are mandatory for the <A> tag.

NAME= The NAME= attribute specifies the name of a specific destination within your HTML document. The name tag is used for what are called *reference links*. These links show at the top of the Web document and reference text later on in the document.

NAME="kids"

Will refer to the section named "kids" later in the document.

REL= The REL= attribute indicates the relationship between the document and another document on the same Web server.

REV= The REV= attribute is similar to the REL= attribute but specifies the relationship from the related document back to its base/original document.

TARGET= The TARGET= attribute specifies a specific window that will open up when the hypertext link is selected. This will be an additional window to the one you have open currently.

TITLE= The TITLE= attribute allows users to preview the title of the document that is hypertext linked prior to actually connecting to and loading the document.

STEP-BY-STEP INSTRUCTIONS FOR BUILDING HYPERTEXT LINKS

CREATING AN INTERNAL LINK (WITH TEXT)

You will be creating many internal links within your Web. These links refer you to and from HTML documents stored on your Web server, from one part of your Web site to another, and from general to more detailed information. To do this, create a text phrase that describes where you will find yourself if you choose that link. Follow the steps below to create an internal text link:

Step 1: Decide on a short text phrase that will represent the link.

Internet Tutorials for Teens

Step 2: Put <A> tags around the text.

<A>Internet Tutorials for Teens**</A>**

Step 3: Inside the first <A> tag, add the file name of the locally stored HTML document (in quotation marks).

<A"teens.html">Internet Tutorials for Teens**</A>**

Note: If the file "teens.html" resides in a different directory than the file containing this link, you must include the complete path to that file.

<A"tutorials/teens.html">Internet Tutorials for Teens**</A>**

Step 4: Finally, inside the first <A> tag, insert HREF= before the HTML document name. (HREF= indicates that what follows it is a hypertext link.)

<A HREF= "teens.html">Internet Tutorials for Teens**</A>**

Result: The phrase will appear as an underlined, highlighted, or colored hypertext link on your Web page. When you select it, you will be connected to and view the HTML document stored on your Web server.

Internet Tutorials for Teens

CREATING AN EXTERNAL LINK (WITH TEXT)

You will also want to add external links to your Web pages. These links can point to HTML documents stored on computers anywhere in the world. When you click on external links you will be leaving your Web site and connecting somewhere else. To do this, first create a text phrase that describes where (outside of your Web site) you will find yourself if you choose that link. The process of creating an external link is very similar to, but not identical to, creating an internal link. Follow the steps below to create an external text link:

Step 1: Decide on a short phrase that will represent the link.

WebTeens

Step 2: Put <A> tags around the text.

<A>WebTeens**</A>**

Step 3: Inside the first <A> tag, add the URL (surrounded by quotation marks).

<A"http://www.oplin.lib.oh.us/EDUCATE/WEBTEENS/ index.html">WebTeens**</A>**

Step 4: Finally, inside the first <A> tag, insert HREF= before the document name.

<A HREF="http://www.oplin.lib.oh.us/EDUCATE/WEBTEENS/ index.html">WebTeens**</A>**

Result: The phrase will appear as an underlined, highlighted, or colored hypertext link on your Web page. When you select it, you will be connected to, and view, the WebTeen page stored on OPLIN's computer in Columbus Ohio.

WebTeens

CREATING A LINK (WITH A GRAPHIC)

Instead of just using words to represent a link, you can also let a picture do the job instead. Graphics can make your Web pages more appealing. Many Web sites use graphics to help you quickly select particular tools or information (e.g., your online catalog, specific collections) or go back to the site's home page.

The process of creating a graphic link bears some similarity to creating a text link, but is slightly more complex. First, you need to prepare and load an image onto your Web server. You can either scan and size your own pictures or use CD-ROM or Web-based graphic libraries. (Try browsing Yahoo! and other Web indexes under terms like "art" or "graphics" to locate Web "clip art" collections.)

This book does not discuss how to scan, size, or load graphics onto your Web server. How you do this depends on your computer, your scanning equipment, and the type of computer that acts as your Web server. The details of how to scan and size pictures and graphics can be found in books in Appendix B. Follow the steps below to create graphic links.

Step 1: Decide on the graphic that will represent the link.

Step 2: Either download a graphic from the Web or CD-ROM, or scan it. Next, convert it to a Web-usable graphic file format (e.g., JPEG, GIF), size it, name it, and store it on your Web server.

Step 3: Type the graphic's name and surround it with quotation marks.

"webteen.jpg"

Step 4: Add IMG SRC= (which indicates that the link is a graphic file) and surround the text with angle brackets. (IMG is the HTML tag and SRC= is its attribute. Both parts let browsers know that the link is to an image, not text.)

<IMG SRC="webteen.jpg">

Step 5: Put <A> tags around the whole thing.

<A><IMG SRC="webteen.jpg"></A>

Step 6: Inside the first <A> tag, add the name of document or URL you want retrieved, surround it with quotation marks, then add HREF=.

<A HREF="teens.html"><IMG SRC="webteen.jpg"></A>

Result: The picture, surrounded by a colored line, will appear as a hypermedia link on your Web page. When you select it, you will be connected to WebTeens (see Figure 2–1.).

Figure 2–1: Graphic Used as a Hypertext Link

CREATING A GRAPHIC LINK FOR USERS WITH SLOW MODEMS OR TEXT-ONLY WEB ACCESS

When you use a graphic link, those people using text-based browsers like Lynx (or people with slow modems who have to turn off graphics to get a Web page to load quickly) are at a disadvantage because they can't see your graphics. Instead of a picture, they see the generic message [IMAGE]. This doesn't give them any idea what they are missing.

There is a way to provide them with a text description of the graphic they can't see. (e.g., [Honor Library Logo], [Picture of a Cat]). Adding customized graphic descriptions is quite simple. The process is almost identical to creating a graphic link with one extra step added to create the customized message in brackets. Follow the steps below to create text-friendly graphic link:

Step 1: Decide on the graphic that will represent the link. Download it, scan, name, save, and store it on your Web server (see Figure 2–2.).

oplin.jpg

Step 2: Place the graphic name in quotation marks, add IMG SRC= and surround it with angle brackets.

<IMG SRC="oplin.jpg"**>**

Step 3: Add ALT= and the customized text description of the graphic in square brackets, surrounded by quotation marks. (ALT= is an optional attribute of the <IMG> tag that indicates that there is an "alternative" description of the graphic.)

<IMG SRC="oplin.jpg"**ALT=**[OPLIN logo]**>**

Step 4: Put <A> tags around the whole thing.

<A><IMG SRC="oplin.jpg"**ALT=**[OPLIN logo]**></A>**

Step 5: Inside the first <A> tag add the HTML document name or URL you want retrieved, surround it with quotation marks and add HREF=.

<A HREF="http://www.oplin.lib.oh.us/"**><IMG SRC=**"oplin.jpg"**ALT=**[OPLIN logo] **></A>**

Hint: This is especially useful for visitors using slower modem connections.

Result: Visitors with a graphical browser, with the graphics turned on, will see the picture link. Visitors with a graphical browser set to delay loading graphics until after the text has loaded, can read the ALT= description to decide if it is worth waiting for the graphic to load. Visitors using text-based browsers will view the text description of the graphic.

CREATING A LINK (WITH A GRAPHIC AND TEXT)

Often it is wise to give the people who visit your Web site choices. Some people prefer pictures and others prefer words. You can satisfy them both by creating links in both picture and text form. This process is a combination of the text and graphic steps described previously. Follow the steps below to create both a picture and text link to the same HTML document:

Step 1: Decide on the text phrase that will represent the link.

   OPLIN Homepage

Step 2: Decide on a graphic that will also represent the link. Download it, scan, name, save, and store it on your Web server.

Step 3: Place the graphic name in quotation marks, add IMG SRC= and surround the whole thing in angle brackets.

   <IMG SRC="oplin.jpg"**>**

Step 4: Add the short text phrase.

   <IMG SRC="oplin.jpg"**>**OPLIN Homepage

Step 5: Put <A> tags around the whole thing.

   <A><IMG SRC="oplin.jpg"**>**OPLIN Homepage**</A>**

Step 6: Inside the first <A> tag add the HTML document name or URL you want retrieved, surround it with quotation marks and then add HREF=.

   <A HREF="oplin.html"**><IMG SRC=**"oplin.jpg"**>**OPLIN Homepage**</A>**

Result: You will see a picture (oplin.jpg) surrounded by a colored line as well as underlined, highlighted, or colored text (OPLIN Homepage). When you choose either one, you will be connected to the OPLIN Homepage.

 OPLIN Homepage

CREATING A LINK THAT CONNECTS TO A SECTION OF TEXT WITHIN YOUR WEB DOCUMENT

When you have a lot of information to provide, or a long list of annotated links you want visitors to look at, your Web document can get pretty long. This means that visitors must scroll through lots of stuff before finding what they want. One way you can handle this is to organize text or links into subject/topical groupings and use "reference links" to take visitors directly down to the information they are seeking. Reference links are placed in a list near the top of a Web page, before the actual content starts. (Sort of like a chapter index.) When a visitor clicks on any one of them, they're routed immediately down through your document to where the information is located. To try out reference links in action, visit OPLIN's WebTots page at *http://www.oplin.lib.oh.us/ WEBTOTS/.* To create text reference links:

> **Hint:** Reference links are great for visitors who are not experienced mouse users, because they don't have to struggle using a scroll bar.

Step 1: Decide on the short text phrase that will represent the link

> Learn to Read

Step 2: Put <A> tags around the text.

> **<A>**Learn to Read**</A>**

Step 3: Inside the first <A> tag, add the name of the "mother" document in quotation marks. (In other words, if the larger document you are subdividing is named "webtots.html" then that is what you put here.)

> **<A**"webtots.html">Learn to Read**</A>**

Step 4: Inside the first <A> tag, insert HREF= before the document name.

> **<A HREF=**"webtots.html">Learn to Read**</A>**

Step 5: To create the reference, insert the pound sign (#) after the file name and then the name of the section you want to link to.

> **<A HREF=**"webtots.html#Read">Learn to Read**</A>**

You've just completed the first part of the reference. Next you'll have to add a tag to the section of text you want the above link to reference.

Step 6: Locate the section of text, or group of links that you want the reference link to jump to when a visitor clicks on it. Look for text that identifies that section (See Figures 2–3 and 2–4.).

<B>Learn to Read**</B>**

Step 7: Add <A> tags in brackets and add the NAME= attribute inside it, then add the name of the section (the same name as behind the # sign in the reference link.)

<A NAME="Read"**><B>**Learn to Read**</B>**

Result: When a visitor clicks on the reference link, the NAME= section of text will be retrieved and displayed on the screen. It's that simple!

WHAT'S NEW   FIND IT   HELP!

ABOUT OH! KIDS   TALK TO OPLIN

OH! KIDS PAGE   OPLIN PAGE

Alphabet Fun

Animals

Learn to Read

Figure 2–2: Text Used as Reference Link

Learn to Read

🐰 **But That Wasn't The Best Part**
    Read all about the Banana Parade and find out what the
    best part was!

Figure 2–3: Reference Link Redirected to the Proper Text

CREATING A LINK THAT OPENS UP AN E-MAIL WINDOW

This type of link is called a *mailto*. It instructs browsers (if possible) to open a window so that visitors can e-mail you their suggestions or comments. It is often found at the bottom of pages along with information found in the <ADDRESS> tag.

<ADDRESS>
Honor Public Library**
**
Copyright 1998**
**
<HREF="mailto:webmaster@honor.lib.oh.us">webmaster@honor.lib.oh.us
**</A>
**
revised 7/21/98**
**
</ADDRESS>

Honor Public Library
Copyright 1998
webmaster@honor.lib.oh.us
revised 2/21/98

In the example above, clicking on the link webmaster@honor.lib.oh.us opens up an e-mail window.

Hint: Mailto links make it possible for patrons to easily comment on library services, suggest materials that the library purchase, or send messages to library staff members.

CREATING LINKS TO MULTIMEDIA

You can create links to media resources stored on your Web server or located on Web servers anywhere in the world. When you create media links, visitors selecting them will view graphics (e.g., pictures, maps, diagrams), hear speeches and music, or view short video clips (e.g., cartoons, news shorts). The structure of a media link is identical to a text link, with one minor exception. With media links you must include the media format and the size of file in the link description, so that visitors will know how big the media file is and what "helper" software they may need to view or hear it.

<A HREF="libpic.jpeg">Library photo. 120K JPEG**</A>**
<A HREF="circ.mpeg">Check-out video tutorial.**</A>**650K MPEG
<A HREF="speech.au">Welcome from the Director.**</A>**AU format, 392K.

CREATING THUMBNAIL GRAPHIC LINKS

You can also create small versions of graphic images (called *thumbnail images*) and use them as links to full size images (See Figures 2–5 and 2–6.). To do this, first create two versions of the same image using a graphic conversion/sizing program, one full size and one small (less than 5K).

<A HREF="larohkds.gif"**><IMG SRC=**"smohkds.gif"**></A>**

Hint: There are a number of advantages to using thumbnail images. Being small in size, thumbnail images load quickly. They also allow you to view the image before deciding whether or not to view the larger image.

Figure 2–4: Large Graphic

Figure 2–5: Thumbnail Graphic Used as a Hypertext Link

TAGS THAT CREATE IMAGEMAPS

See Chapter 3 to learn how *Mapedit* uses these tags to create imagemaps for your Web pages. (Since you will be using imagemap software to create your first imagemap, we will only briefly discuss what to do. We assume once you use a nifty program like *Mapedit*, you won't want to create an imagemap the older, harder way, using only HTML tags.)

MAP TAG <MAP>

The <MAP> </MAP> tag pair identifies an imagemap. Each map is required to have a unique name. The accompanying <AREA>tag defines what the imagemap will look like and what it will link to.

An Attribute You Can Use with <MAP> Tags

NAME= *Mandatory* The NAME= attribute specifies the name of the specific imagemap.

AREA TAG <AREA>

The single <AREA> tag contains all the detailed information about the imagemap. Each linked section of an imagemap will have a separate <AREA> tag that includes specific information about each area of the graphic you are mapping. (See Chapter 3 for a complete example of the Plumfield Library's imagemap tags.)

Attributes You Can Use with <AREA> Tags

ALT= The ALT= tag describes the imagemap for a visitor using a text-only browser.

> **ALT=[Reference Department]**

COORDS= The COORDS= attribute specifies the numerical coordinates (separated by commas) of the area to be linked to a specific URL.

HREF= The HREF= attribute specifies the URL to which the coordinates are linked.

NOHREF The NOHREF attribute specifies an area of an imagemap that has no defined URL attached to it.

SHAPE= The SHAPE= attribute specifies the shape of an imagemap area. The shape chosen affects how coordinates are expressed. The most common used shape is RECT (short for rectangle), however you can also use CIRCLE or POLY . . . for irregular shapes.

TAGS THAT CREATE TABLES

If you need assistance, see Chapter 4 for details on how to use these tags to create Web-based tables.

TABLE TAG <TABLE>

The <TABLE> </TABLE> tag pair identifies the start and end to a table.

Attributes You Can Use with <TABLE> Tags

ALIGN= The ALIGN= attribute specifies three options LEFT, RIGHT, CENTER. Use them to specify whether you want a table aligned with the left or right margins, or centered on a browser screen.

BGCOLOR= The BGCOLOR= attribute specifies the hexadecimal color that will be used for table's background color. (See Appendix C for a listing of all hexadecimal colors.)

> **BGCOLOR="FFCC00"**

Will create a light yellow background.

Hint: Tables
display with a
default border,
which is set to 1
pixel. If you don't
want a border, set
the value to 0.

BORDER= The BORDER= attribute specifies a border for the table. The value is expressed in pixels.

BORDER=3

Draws a border line 3 pixels wide.

CELLPADDING= The CELLPADDING= attribute specifies the white space left between the edge of a table cell and cell text. The padding relates to both horizontal and vertical white space. The value is expressed in pixels.

Hint: Cellpadding
affects how text
flows inside a table
column, so be
sure to experiment
with the pixel
value.

CELLPADDING=10

Means that there will be 10 pixels of white space on all sides of the text.

CELLSPACING= The CELLSPACING= attribute specifies in pixels the width of the shaded lines between different table cells. Use this attribute to visually separate date and create more white space between cell text.

CELLSPACING=3

Puts a three pixel wide space between individual table cells.

RULES= The RULES= attribute specifies the type of lines that appear in a table. The value NONE means that there will be no lines dividing cells inside the table. The value BASIC draws lines between the table head, table foot and table body. The value ROWS draws horizontal lines between all rows in a table. The value COLS draws vertical lines between each table column. The value ALL draws both vertical and horizontal lines between each table cell.

Hint: Using
WIDTH= per-
centages allows
your browser to
resize the table
based on the width
of the computer
screen it displays
on, whereas using
pixels keeps the
size of the table
constant
regardless of the
screen size.

WIDTH= The WIDTH= attribute specifies the width of table cells. The value can be either expressed exactly in pixels or approximately in percentages, based on the width of the whole table.

HSPACE= Netscape only The HSPACE= attribute specifies how much white space you want on either side of the table. The value is expressed in pixels.

HSPACE=15

Will create 15 pixels of white space on either side of your table.

VALIGN= Netscape only The VALIGN= attribute has four values, TOP, MIDDLE, BOTTOM, BASELINE. It specifies where you want the table to display on the page.

VSPACE= Netscape only The VSPACE= attribute specifies how much white space you want above or below the table. The value is expressed in pixels.

VSPACE=15

Will create 15 pixels of white space above and below your table.

CAPTION TAG <CAPTION>

The <CAPTION> </CAPTION> tag pair identifies the text that will form a table caption.

An Attribute You Can Use with <CAPTION> Tags

ALIGN= The ALIGN= attribute specifies whether the table's caption is above or below the table. The two values are TOP and BOTTOM.

TABLE ROW TAG <TR>

The <TR> </TR> tag pair creates a single row in a table. Each row will contain a header, expressed by the <TH> tag and data, and individual cells expressed by the <TD> tag. Each table will contain multiple sets of <TR> tags that define each row in a table.

Attributes You Can Use with <TR> Tags

ALIGN= The ALIGN= attribute allows three options LEFT, RIGHT, CENTER. Use it to specify how text aligns itself within a table row.

VALIGN= The VALIGN= attribute allows four options TOP, BOTTOM, MIDDLE, and BASELINE. This attribute specifies how the text lines up vertically inside a row.

TABLE HEADING TAG <TH>

The <TH> </TH> tag pair identifies text as a table heading. Table headings identify the contents of data cells. They can display horizontally and/or vertically and can span more than one table cell. Attributes allow you to set up both text and cells within table headings.

Attributes You Can Use with <TH> Tags

ALIGN= The ALIGN= attribute specifies three options LEFT, RIGHT, CENTER. Use it to indicate how you want the text aligned horizontally inside each heading cell.

COLSPAN= The COLSPAN= attribute specifies when you want to create a table heading that spans more than one column. The value is the number of columns you want the heading to span.

COLSPAN=2

Means that a single table heading would span the two columns directly below it.

NOWRAP The NOWRAP attribute specifies that the contents of the cell should not word wrap, but display as set up.

ROWSPAN= The ROWSPAN= attribute specifies that a table heading should span more than one row. The value is the number of rows you want the heading to span.

ROWSPAN=2

Means that a single table heading would span over the two rows directly to the right.

VALIGN= The VALIGN= attribute allows four options TOP, BOTTOM, MIDDLE, and BASELINE. This attribute controls how the text lines up vertically within each heading cell.

TABLE DATA TAG <TD>

The <TD> </TD> tag pair identifies a table data cell. Table data tags are always placed within Table Heading Tags <TH>. Data cells contain individual pieces of information that display under or next to table headings, which help organize and clarify the data cell elements. Attributes set up text within individual data cells and cell placement inside their related table heading.

Attributes You Can Use with <TD> Tags

ALIGN= The ALIGN= attribute specifies three options LEFT, RIGHT, CENTER. Use them to indicate how you want the text aligned horizontally within each data cell.

COLSPAN= The COLSPAN= attribute specifies that a data cell is to span more than one column directly below it. The value is the number of columns you want the data cell to span.

NOWRAP The NOWRAP attribute specifies that the contents of the cell should not word wrap, but display as set up.

ROWSPAN= The ROWSPAN= attribute specifies that a data cell should span more that one row. The value is the number of rows you want the cell to span.

ROWSPAN=2

Means that a single data cell would span over the two row cells directly to the right of it.

VALIGN= The VALIGN= attribute specifies four options TOP, BOTTOM, MIDDLE, and BASELINE. It controls how text lines up vertically within each data cell.

TAGS THAT CREATE FRAMES

If you need assistance, see Chapter 5 for examples of how to create Web pages with frames.

FRAME SET TAG <FRAMESET>

The <FRAMESET> </FRAMESET> tag pair specifies that an HTML document contains frames and defines how individual frames will display. The <FRAMESET> tag acts a lot like (and substitutes for) the <BODY> tag in an HTML document containing frames. Multiple <FRAMESET> tags can be used within a document.

Attributes You Can Use with <FRAMESET> Tags

COLS= The COLS= attribute specifies the number of frames that divide a Web page vertically. The value can be either a specific pixel size or an approximate size expressed as percentages of the full screen.

ROWS= The ROWS= attribute specifies the number of frames that divide the page horizontally. The value can be either a specific pixel size, or an approximate size expressed as percentages of the full screen.

BORDER= The BORDER= attribute specifies the width of the frame border in pixels. Setting the BORDER= value to "0" creates a borderless frame.

FRAME TAG <FRAME>

The <FRAME> </FRAME> specifies an individual frame within a framed HTML document. The <FRAMESET> tag contains all <FRAME> tag pairs. Attributes define the text that will display in the frame and how the frame itself will display.

Attributes You Can Use with <FRAME> Tags

NAME= The NAME= attribute defines the frame using a unique name.

NAME="bob"

Will create a frame named "bob."

NORESIZE The NORESIZE attribute locks individual frames to the preset size/percentages, so visitors can't resize them by using a mouse to drag the border of a frame larger or smaller.

SCROLLING= The SCROLLING= attribute specifies whether a scroll bar displays along with a frame. There are three values for this attribute. YES specifies that scroll bars will display, NO specifies that scrolls bars won't display or AUTO, which displays

Hint: When using COLS= percentages, frames will resize to fit different size computer screens, whereas pixels preset the size of the frame regardless of the screen size. This can result in frames that scroll off the bottom of the screen.

Hint: When using ROWS= percentages, frames will resize to fit different size computer screens. Pixels preset the size of the frame regardless of the screen size and often create frames that scroll off the screen to the right.

Hint: Use NORESIZE when you want total control over how your framed Web page looks.

a scroll bar only when one is needed. NO is not generally a good option, if a scroll bar is needed. AUTO is the best value to choose.

SRC= The SRC= attribute specifies the URL of the HTML document you want to display inside the frame.

> **FRAME SRC=**"http://www.ohionet.org"

ANCHOR TAG <A>

Anchor tags <A></A> identify hypertext links and can be used with frames to specify a specific frame you want a link to connect to.

An Attribute You Can Use with <A> Tags

TARGET= The TARGET= attribute specifies a specific window name that will open up when the hypertext link is selected. This will be an additional frame/window to the one you have open currently.

> **<A HREF=**"main.html"**TARGET=**"content">Main Page**</A>

NO FRAMES TAG <NOFRAMES>

> **Hint:** It's a good idea to provide visitors with both frames and no-frames versions of your Web site; some visitors just don't like frames, others have to use the no-frames version because their browser doesn't support frames.

The <NOFRAMES> </NOFRAMES> tag pair specifies the text of a message to visitors who aren't using a frames-capable browser (e.g., early versions of graphical browsers and text-based browsers). The message can also include a hypertext link to a no-frames version of your Web site.

TAGS THAT CREATE FORMS

If you need assistance, see Chapter 6 for examples of how to create Web-based forms.

FORM TAG <FORM>

The <FORM> </FORM> tag pair specifies that an HTML document contains a form. Attributes indicate how information submitted via the form will be processed.

Attributes You Can Use with <FORM> Tags

ACTION= The ACTION= attribute specifies the CGI script on your Web server, so that it can process the information submitted via the form.

> **ACTION=**"http://www.xyz.com/cgi-bin/hi.pl"

The URL is the server name, the directory name—usually CGI-BIN—and the PERL script name (hi.pl).

METHOD= The METHOD= attribute specifies how information is to be submitted to your Web server for processing. There are two values GET and POST. GET is the preferred value because it is supported by more Web servers.

INPUT TAG <INPUT>

The single <INPUT> tag specifies the place where visitors can submit information via a Web-based form. There can be multiple <INPUT> tags in each form. Attributes identify how the input area will display.

Attributes You Can Use with <INPUT> Tags

ALIGN= The ALIGN= attribute here is used just like the ALIGN= attribute with the <IMG> tag. The first option LEFT places the input area near the left margin. The RIGHT option places the input area near the right margin. The next option places the input area in relation to surrounding text. The TOP option places the top of the input area in line with text. The MIDDLE option centers the input area vertically with the text, and the BOTTOM option aligns the bottom of the input area with the text.

MAXLENGTH= The MAXLENGTH= attribute specifies the maximum length for input. MAXLENGTH= is used in conjunction with the SIZE= attribute.

NAME= The NAME= attribute specifies a unique name for each form input element, so that your Web server knows what to do with it.

NAME="normal"

Means that that element is named "normal."

SIZE= The SIZE= attribute specifies the size of the input area. The number represents the number of characters that the input area will hold without scrolling.

TYPE= The TYPE= attribute specifies different types of input gathering options, which all display differently. Some of the values are CHECKBOX, PASSWORD, RADIO, SUBMIT, TEXT, HIDDEN, RESET. (See Chapter 6 for a fuller explanation and examples of these input types.)

VALUE= The VALUE= attribute specifies different input elements, such as radio buttons and checkboxes. The attribute identifies the information to be submitted with each radio button or checkbox choice.

VALUE="NO"
VALUE="YES"

Each sends a different answer to the Web server.

Hint: You'll want to use text areas when you want visitors to give you their comments that might be many lines or even paragraph long. You can also use this area for information like mailing addresses.

TEXT AREA TAG <TEXTAREA>

The <TEXTAREA> </TEXTAREA> tag pair specifies an area where visitors can key in a free-form note, using a text box.

Attributes You Can Use with <TEXTAREA> Tags

COLS= The COLS= attribute specifies the horizontal size of the input area, expressed as a number of characters.

COLS=40

Creates an input area that will be 40 characters wide.

NAME= The NAME= attribute specifies a unique name for a text area, so that your Web server knows what to do with it.

NAME="address"

Means that the text input area is named "address."

ROWS= The ROWS= attribute specifies the vertical size of the input area, expressed as a number of characters.

ROWS=5

Creates an input area that will take up to five lines of text.

SELECT TAG <SELECT>

The <SELECT> </SELECT> tag pair creates a pull-down list, from which a visitor can choose one option. The <SELECT> tag is used with the <OPTIONS> tag.

Attributes You Can Use with <SELECT> Tags

MULTIPLE The MULTIPLE attribute allows you to make multiple selections from a pull-down list.

NAME= The NAME= attribute specifies a unique name for each pull-down input element, so that your Web server knows what to do with it.

NAME="Public"

Hint: If no SIZE= attribute is used, the list displays all the choices at once.

Means that the pull-down element is named "Public."

SIZE= The SIZE= attribute specifies the number of pull-down elements that display. If the SIZE= attribute is used, the list will be scrollable and the attribute value will indicate how many lines will display before scrolling is necessary.

OPTION TAG <OPTION>

The single <OPTION> tag is used with the <SELECT> tag. It identifies each choice in the pull-down menu created by the <SELECT> tag.

OPTION=Public libraries
OPTION=School libraries

Will create two pull-down options, one displaying "Public libraries" and the other "School libraries."

Attributes You Can Use with <OPTION> Tags

VALUE= The VALUE= tag can be used two ways. First, to submit the value that goes along with the pull-down option selected. Second, and more commonly, if the first <OPTION> tag is set to VALUE= " ", and followed by instructional text, the tag will display selection instructions for visitors.

<OPTION VALUE= > " " Select one item from the list

3

Creating Imagemaps

*If you need assistance, see **Chapter 2** for imagemap tags and attributes.*

WHAT IS AN IMAGEMAP?

An imagemap is a graphic image that contains hypertext links. They can send a visitor to your Web site to different Web pages depending on the section of the graphic that the visitors clicks. Imagemaps allow one image to serve as a visual map to your entire Web site. When created correctly, imagemaps look professional and help visitors to easily navigate your Web site. For all these reasons imagemaps are very popular "add-ons."

ACCESS CONSIDERATIONS

Before creating an imagemap, it's important to consider the impact that one will have on the visitors to your Web site. Remember, that by using imagemaps, visitors with text-only or older browser versions will be unable to view your imagemap. Therefore, provide an alternate access method for these visitors . . . simply provide text links that duplicate the links provided in your imagemap (See Figure 3–1.). (Usually located just below the imagemap.)

IMAGEMAP TYPES

There are three types of imagemaps currently in use: CERN, NCSA, and Client-Side (CSIM). Both CERN and NCSA imagemaps are server-side imagemaps, which depend on a Web server for processing and delivering imagemap requests for a visitor.

Reference | Circulation | Special Collections

Figure 3–1: Imagemap Layout and Design

A SERVER-SIDE IMAGEMAP WORKS LIKE THIS:

1. A visitor clicks on a specific area of an imagemap.
2. The location where the visitor clicked is sent to the remote server.
3. The server identifies the location of the click.
4. The server sends the visitor the information linked to that location.

A client-side imagemap uses a visitor's browser to identify and deliver information. After the page is initially loaded there is no further interaction with the Web server. This reduces the four-step process used by server-side imagemaps to a more efficient two-step process.

A CLIENT-SIDE IMAGEMAP WORKS THIS WAY:

1. A visitor clicks on a specific area of an imagemap.
2. The visitor's Web browser identifies and delivers the information requested by the click.

Client-side imagemaps are part of the trend to move as much Web page processing as possible from the Web server to the visitor's computer and browser.

STEP 1: SELECT A GRAPHIC

The process of creating an imagemap is rather simple. First, you'll need a digitized graphic. It will need to be saved in a graphic format viewable on the Web (either .GIF or .JPG). There are a number of graphics programs available for creating digital images. These packages range from fully featured commercial products such as: Adobe Photoshop, and Corel Draw to quality shareware programs such as Paint Shop Pro. There are also Web-based "clip art" sites where you can download existing graphics.

Hint: Be wary of Web sites that don't respect the copyright law!

STEP 2: SELECT AREAS

Once you have selected a graphic, you can begin to create your imagemap. First, determine the areas of the map that will be "active"—those, that when clicked will send a visitor to another document.

Hint: It's a good idea to sketch the different areas of your imagemap, indicating the links related to each part.

STEP 3: PLOT THE MAP

After you have determined and sketched out the areas of your imagemap that will be active, you'll need to "plot" the map's x, y coordinates. When imagemaps were first introduced they were plotted by hand, a very time-consuming and inefficient process. Today, hand plotting is no longer required. Now imagemap creation programs do all the plotting "grunt work" quickly and simply.

The program that you will be using to create your first imagemap is a shareware product called *Mapedit*. It will help you quickly create imagemaps and will save you hours of hand-plotting headaches.

STEP-BY-STEP INSTRUCTIONS FOR USING *MAPEDIT*

To create your first imagemap, you'll need to install the Mapedit *software found in the Programs directory on the CD-ROM. Read the installation instructions in the* **MEreadme.txt file** *found in the Text directory on the CD-ROM.*

<u>Step 1:</u> After you have installed *Mapedit,* start the program. The following screen should appear:

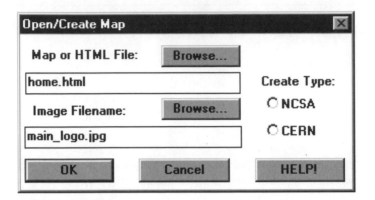

Figure 3–2: Getting Started with *Mapedit*

<u>Step 2:</u> You will be asked to supply the name of an HTML document that will contain your imagemap. This file must contain a reference to the graphic that will create your imagemap. A list of all graphics contained in that document will appear. Select the image you'll use to create your imagemap.

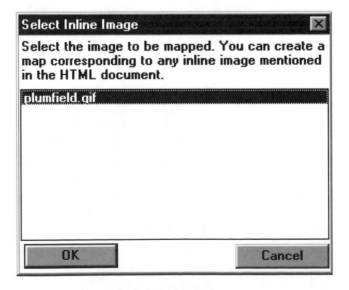

Figure 3–3: *Mapedit* Image List

Next, you'll define the areas of your imagemap. To accomplish this you'll use the *Mapedit* shape tools (square, circle, and polygon). Select the shape tool that you want to use.

Figure 3–4: *Mapedit* Shape Tools

Step 3: Click on an area of the image where you want to start defining coordinates, then click and hold the left mouse button as you drag it around to highlight the desired area. Click the mouse again to complete the shape.

Step 4: Next, you'll be prompted to supply a URL and other information about the area that you have just defined. Complete the first two fields labeled: "URL for clicks on this object" and "Alternate text."

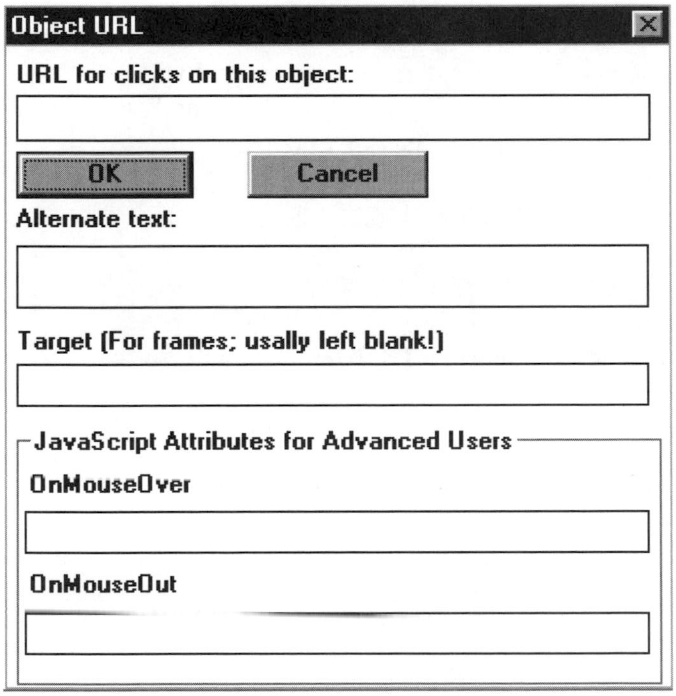

Figure 3–5: *Mapedit* Area Information

Step 5: After you have completed your first "active" area, move to the other areas of the imagemap and define their shapes. As you define each area, *Mapedit* will automatically identify and store the coordinates of the areas that you select.

Hint: In most cases this should be the same URL of the Web page that contains the imagemap.

Step 6: After you have defined all "active" areas, select the "FILE" menu and click on "Edit Default URL." You will be prompted to enter a URL that will be activated when an "undefined" area of the graphic is clicked on.

Step 7: After you finish providing this information, "Save" your first imagemap file.

Result: All of the necessary HTML tags will be created by *Mapedit* and added to your imagemap.

SAMPLE HTML DOCUMENT PRODUCED BY *MAPEDIT*

```
<HTML>
<HEAD>
<TITLE>
Plumfield University Library Home Page
</TITLE>
</HEAD>
<BODY BGCOLOR="FFFFFF">
<IMG SRC="plumfield.gif" USEMAP="#plumfield">
<MAP NAME="plumfield">
<AREA SHAPE="rect" ALT="Reference Department" COORDS="48,183,143,204"
HREF="http://www.plumfield.edu/library/ref.html">
<AREA SHAPE="rect" ALT="Circulation Department" COORDS="135,207,243,224"
HREF="http://www.plumfield.edu/library/circ.html">
<AREA SHAPE="rect" ALT="Special Collections" COORDS="240,230,404,242"
HREF="http://www.plumfield.edu/library/spec.html">
<AREA SHAPE="rect" HREF="http://www.plumfield.edu/library" COORDS="0,0,449,249">
</MAP>
</BODY>
</HTML>
```

The HTML document produced by *Mapedit* is not too difficult to understand. There is the opening map tag that contains the name of the map <MAPNAME= "X">. The next set of tags define the areas of the map. These tags can be broken down into the following parts:

AREA—opening of the area tag
SHAPE=RECT—the type of shape defined
COORDS="30,180,150,210"—plotted x,y coordinates for the defined area
HREF=http://www.plumfield.edu/library/ref.html—link to be displayed when an "inactive" area is selected.
ALT="Reference Department"—Alternative text of for non-graphical browsers.

The last tag produced by *Mapedit* is the closing map tag </MAP>. (For a further explanation of these tags, see Chapter 2.)

TEST YOUR KNOWLEDGE

Create your own imagemap using *Mapedit*. It should contain the following elements:

- A minimum of three areas linking to other locations on the Web.
- A default URL that should be set to the Web page that contains the imagemap.
- Text links for visitors with non-graphical browsers.

4

Creating Tables

If you need assistance, see Chapter 2 for table tags and attributes.

WHAT ARE TABLES?

Tables are arrangements of text into columns and rows. This text is identified by various HTML tags that display and arrange the text.

Here are some reasons why you might want to use tables on your library Web pages:

- You want to display data aligned both horizontally and vertically on a page. (Great for your library statistics.)
- You want to display a list of links that display in both columns and rows. (Visitors see all the links in a compact bunch, without having to use the scroll bar.)
- You want to make sure that text lines up directly over and under other text. (Good for financial statements, contributions, and budget allocations.)
- You want to change the arrangement of text on your Web page from purely vertical to either horizontal or a combination of both. (Great for staff directory information.)
- You want to arrange groups of small graphics either horizontally, vertically, or both. (Good for simple graphic navigation groupings for your Web page.)

However, tables can disrupt the overall graphic look of a Web page. For a simple table example visit *http://www.kcpl.lib.mo.us/search/chart.html*.

Setting up tables from scratch is somewhat more complicated than setting up HTML lists. Tables, however, are not really all that hard to figure out, once you understand basic table structure. There are HTML creation programs that will set up tables for you

Hint: People look at table information before they look at other kinds of text. If the table you create is less important than other information on the page, or if it is large or very complex, you should consider creating a link to the table rather than putting it directly on your Web page.

without you really having to know how the tables are built. We recommend that you learn to build tables from scratch in order to learn how they are structured and how various table attributes affect both the table itself and the text inside each table cell. Once you understand how tables work, then try building one using the table building sub-programs found in many of the most recent HTML editors.

ALTERNATIVES TO TABLES

Hint: Use <PRE> to line text up in columns or rows and it will display it as you typed it. <PRE> is also a quick way to create tables and is appropriate for information that will display for only a short time— information that will change from day to day, or week to week.

Before you start learning how to build tables, consider some other HTML alternatives to tables.

First, you can use <PRE> tags. Text inside these <PRE> tags will display as you type it, white space included. The only problem with using <PRE> tags is that text will display in Courier (typewriter-like) font. If you are displaying information that will remain the same from month to month, setting it up in a table, or one of the other table alternatives, is more appropriate and much more attractive.

Second, you can use various types of HTML lists. If the number of items is quite short, it is less complicated and often more attractive to list items rather than putting them in a table. However, if your list is long and you want as much information as possible to display on a visitor's computer screen, then creating a table might be a better choice.

Third, you can use an image rather than a table. To do this, create tabular information using a word processor or spreadsheet program, save it as a graphic, and then include it as an inline graphic on your Web page. (No matter what size computer screen or browser version a visitor uses, the graphic will always look the same—although graphics can take longer to load. Use the ALT= attribute to provide information for visitors with text-only browsers.)

PARTS OF A TABLE

Figure 4–1 illustrates the various parts of a table. The first part (Honor Public Library), which displays above the table, is called the *caption* and is identified by the <CAPTION> tag pair. The first part of the table (World Wide Web Resources) is called the table heading and is identified by the <TH> tag pair. Each of the individual boxes in the table are called *table cells,* including the box with the heading World Wide Web Resources. Inside each of the cells are table data (Science, Libraries). Table data is identified by the <TD> tag pair.

THE <TABLE> TAG

Hint: Whether you use a table border or not is mostly a design consideration. View tables both ways and decide which looks best on your Web page.

Let's start out by looking at the first tag <TABLE> in more detail. The <TABLE> tag pair identifies text as part of a table and displays it as such. Attributes affect how the table itself displays. The first attribute is the BORDER attribute. As you can see from the two examples in Figure 4–1, the first table contains the border attribute, the second one does not. In addition, the BORDER attribute also can be defined as a numerical value. BORDER=3 creates a table border 3 pixels wide. (The default border is 1 pixel wide.)

You can also use the BGCOLOR= attribute and a hexadecimal color value (see Appendix D for color values) to create a colored background for tables. The ALIGN= attribute allows you to left/right justify, or center a table on a page. The WIDTH= attribute specifies how wide a table will be. You can set the table's width to a set number of pixels by (WIDTH=50). If you specify the width as a pixel number, the size of the table will not vary no matter what size computer screen it is displayed on. You can also specify the table width as a percentage of the total screen.

Hint: If you set the width to 75 percent, the table will stretch to 75 percent of a 15" screen or 75 percent of a 21" computer screen.

Honor Public Library

World Wide Web Resources			
Art-Music	Business	Education	Genealogy
Government	History	Kids Stuff	Libraries
Literature	Science	Sociology	Technology

Honor Public Library

World Wide Web Resources

Art-Music	Business	Education	Genealogy
Government	History	Kids Stuff	Libraries
Literature	Science	Sociology	Technology

Figure 4–1: Parts of a Table, with and without a Border

See the file
4–1.html *in the*
HTML folder on
the CD-ROM for a
copy you can view
with your browser.

Below is the tagging that corresponds to the table with the border. You will want to refer to it when learning about the other table tags.

```
<TABLE BORDER>
<CAPTION><B>Honor Public Library<B></CAPTION>
<TR>
<TH COLSPAN=4>World Wide Web Resources</TH>
</TR>
<TR>
    <TD>Art-Music</TD>
    <TD>Business</TD>
    <TD>Education</TD>
    <TD>Genealogy</TD>
</TR>
<TR>
    <TD>Government</TD>
    <TD>History</TD>
    <TD>Kids Stuff</TD>
    <TD>Libraries</TD>
</TR>
<TR>
    <TD>Literature</TD>
    <TD>Science</TD>
    <TD>Sociology</TD>
    <TD>Technology</TD>
</TR>
</TABLE>
```

THE <CAPTION> TAG

Hint: Captions are optional, and if you don't want a table to have a caption, just leave this tag out. If a table is large, it is best to use a top caption.

The <CAPTION> tag pair specifies the text that is used to describe the table as a whole, or for introductory text. In Figure 4–1 the caption is Honor Public Library. Captions can display at the top or bottom of a table. Use the ALIGN= attribute, with either TOP or BOTTOM to place a caption where you want it. Since a top caption is the default, you only really need to use the ALIGN= attribute when you want to place a caption at the bottom of a table.

THE <TH> TAG

Table headings describe and/or define the table data. The table heading for Figure 4–1 is World Wide Web Resources. Table headings usually display in bold and are centered inside their table cell. Note that the table heading example has an attribute COLSPAN=4. This tells the table header to span across all four columns, and create one long cell with centered text inside. We'll discuss the COLSPAN attribute and additional <TH> tag attributes in more detail when we discuss Figure 4–4.

THE <TD> TAG

Table data goes into the <TD> tag pair. Table data can be numbers, words, and even graphics. Table data is not displayed in bold or centered. The default value is left-justified. In the sample above, we used the default values for the tag. Notice that cell columns vary in width. The width of the row of columns depends on the length of the text in each row. In the sample, we used similar length words to create similar sized columns of cells.

BUILDING A TABLE

Tables are built horizontally, row-by-row, starting from the top and moving to the bottom. Take a look at Figure 4–1 again. Note that each row begins and ends with a <TR> tag, and within each row, moving left to right (but tagged from top to bottom), are individual pieces of information found in each of the <TD> tags.

Note also that each row is separately tagged. (There are three rows of four columns in the above sample. Look at Figure 4–1 again to see how this is reflected in the tagging.) The number of columns are set up automatically based on how many <TD> tags you include in each set of <TH> tags.

In order for a table to work correctly and all the cells line up correctly, each row should have the name number of cells in it. Sometimes, though, you won't have data to put into all the cells. To take care of this situation you can set up empty cells to fill in the space, so the table elements line up correctly. To do this, type in <TH>
</TH> or <TD>
<TD> and a cell will display, but nothing will show inside it. (See Figure 4–4 to see what an empty cell looks like.)

Before you build your first table, sketch what you want it to look like and label each of the table cells, identifying text as headers or data. Start at the top left, at the top row and start creating your table.

ARRANGING DATA IN TABLES

Table headings and table data information can be arranged either horizontally or vertically. Take a look at Figure 4–2 and the tagging sample that goes along with it, to see how each of the two tables are built. In the first sample the first row contains two <TH> tags. In the second table, the first and second rows contain a pair of <TH> and <TD> tags.

Hint: Look back at the tagging in Figure 4–1. Notice that the caption is in bold. We added <B> tags to make it so. Captions are not normally displayed in bold.

Hint: There are attributes that can change both the placement of text and the white space around text. See Chapter 2 for <TD> attribute details.

Hint: There is a way to set up a fixed column size by using the WIDTH= attribute with either <TH> or <TD> tags. See Chapter 2.

Hint: Sketching a table can help keep you from getting confused as to what information goes into what row and data cell. Believe us, each time you build a table, no matter how many you've built before, you'll find it easier with a sketch to work from.

Figure 4–2 is a very simple example of how you can arrange data and header information both horizontally and vertically. See Figure 4–4 for a more complex example . . . we'll discuss it in more detail later.

Library Hours

Weekdays	Weekends
9 AM - 9 PM	9 AM - 5 PM

Library Hours

Weekdays	9 AM - 9 PM
Weekends	9 AM - 5 PM

Figure 4–2: Different Arrangements of Table Data

Here are the two sets of tagging that created the tables above.

*See the file
4–2.html in the
HTML folder on
the CD-ROM for a
copy you can view
with your browser.*

```
<TABLE BORDER>
<CAPTION><B>Library Hours<B></CAPTION>
<TR>
    <TH>Weekdays</TH>
    <TH>Weekends</TH>
</TR>
<TR>
    <TD>9 AM—9 PM</TD>
    <TD>9 AM—5 PM</TD>
</TR>
</TABLE>
```

```
<TABLE BORDER>
<CAPTION><B>Library Hours<B></CAPTION>
<TR>
    <TH>Weekdays</TH>
    <TD>9 AM—9 PM</TD>
</TR>
<TR>
    <TH>Weekends</TH>
    <TD>9 AM—5 PM</TD>
</TR>
</TABLE>
```

ALIGNING INFORMATION IN INDIVIDUAL TABLE CELLS

The <TH> and <TD> tag pairs allow you to align text within each table cell using two attributes: ALIGN= and VALIGN=. ALIGN= specifies the horizontal alignment of information, and VALIGN= the vertical arrangement of information. See Figure 4–3 and the tagging sample that goes along with it, to see how to use these attributes to align text.

Also, see Chapter 2 for information about the CELLPADDING= attribute that is used to create differing amounts of white space around text or graphics inside a table cell.

Hint: You can change the alignment of both table headings (the default is centered both horizontally and vertically) and data cells (the default is aligned left and centered vertically).

Aligned Left	Aligned Center	Aligned Right
9-5	9-5	9-5

Aligned Top	9-5
Aligned Center	9-5
Aligned Bottom	9-5

Figure 4–3: Text Alignment within Table Cells

*See the file **4–3.html** in the HTML folder on the CD-ROM for a copy you can view with your browser.*

The following tagging created the tables above.

```
<TABLE BORDER>
<TR>
    <TH>Aligned Left</TH>
    <TH>Aligned Center</TH>
    <TH>Aligned Right</TH>
</TR>
<TR>
    <TD ALIGN=LEFT>9–5</TD>
    <TD ALIGN=CENTER>9–5</TD>
    <TD ALIGN=RIGHT>9–5</TD>
</TR>
</TABLE>
<TABLE BORDER>
<TR>
    <TH>Aligned<BR>Top</TH>
    <TD VALIGN=TOP>9–5</TD>
</TR>
<TR>
    <TH>Aligned<BR>Center</TH>
    <TD VALIGN=CENTER>9–5</TD>
</TR>
<TR>
    <TH>Aligned<BR>Bottom</TH>
    <TD VALIGN=BOTTOM>9–5</TD>
</TR>
</TABLE>
```

See the file 4–4.html in the HTML folder on the CD-ROM for a copy you can view with your browser.

CREATING A TABLE WITH VARIOUS ELEMENTS

Let's take a look at Figure 4–4 and the accompanying tagging sample to see how to build a table like this.

Welcome to Honor Public Library

		Library Hours		Programs for Patrons
		Weekdays	Weekends	
Main Library	Adult Collection	9 am - 9 pm	9 am - 5 pm	Tues - Story Hour
	Children's Room	9 am - 7 pm	9 am - 5 pm	Wed - Book Club
Southfield Branch		9 am - 7 pm	9 am - 4 pm	Fri - Genealogy Club

Figure 4–4: Table with Various Elements

Here is the tagging that created the table on page 66.

```
<TABLE BORDER>
<CAPTION><B>Welcome to Honor Public Library<B></CAPTION>
<TR>
     <TH ROWSPAN=2 COLSPAN=2><BR></TH>
     <TH COLSPAN=2>Library Hours</TH>
     <TH COLSPAN=2 ROWSPAN=2>Programs<BR>for Patrons</TH>
</TR>
<TR>
     <TH>Weekdays</TH>
     <TH>Weekends</TH>
</TR>
<TR>
     <TH ROWSPAN=2>Main<BR>Library</TH>
     <TD>Adult Collection</TD>
     <TD>9 am—9 pm</TD>
     <TD>9 am—5 pm</TD>
     <TD ROWSPAN=2>Tues—Story Hour<BR>Wed—Book Club</TD>
</TR>
<TR>
     <TD>Children's Room</TD>
     <TD>9 am—7 pm</TD>
     <TD>9 am—5 pm</TD>
</TR>
<TR>
     <TH COLSPAN=2>Southfield Branch</TH>
     <TD>9 am—7 pm</TD>
     <TD>9 am—4 pm</TD>
     <TD>Fri—Genealogy Club</TD>
</TR>
</TABLE>
```

Let's examine the above table row-by row.

- First, note the first row and the empty cell at the top left. (Note especially the <BR> tag that creates an empty cell.) Notice that the empty cell spans vertically down two columns and horizontally across two rows, hence the ROWSPAN=2 and COLSPAN=2 attributes. Take a look at the Programs for Patrons box which is similarly constructed (especially the <BR> tag that breaks the text.) Note also that Library Hours spans two columns, but only one row.
- The second row of this table is easy to miss. It contains the two table headings Weekdays and Weekends. The reason that is all the row contains, is that both of the first row cells to the left and right (blank and Programs for Patrons) affect this

row as well and take care of the space to the left and right of the two heading cells in this row.

- The third row can be confusing when first seen. The first element, the table heading Main Library, is to the left of the table and spans two rows down vertically (just like the last element, Story Hour/Book Club). Note the use of <BR> tags to break text so it flows well in the box area. The rest of the third column is only one row wide and contains information on the adult collection (moving from left to right).
- The first column of the fourth row has already been handled by the third row, which contains Main Library. Also the last two row element Story Hour/Book Club. Hence, the only information in this row has to do with the children's room hours.
- The last row is more straightforward. The table heading Southfield Branch spans two columns (as does the last column, Genealogy Club). The rest is pretty straightforward.

DOING MORE WITH TABLES

Hint: The trick to creating interesting and complex tables has to do with knowing the different tags and attributes, but also being willing to experiment with your table until you get table information to display just the right way. **Warning:** Be sure to thoroughly test all tables you create using different browsers and different size computer screens.

Chapter 2 provides you with most of the attributes associated with table tags. Once you feel comfortable creating a table similar to the one in Figure 4–4, turn to Chapter 2 and start experimenting with <TABLE> attributes like CELLSPACING=, WIDTH=, RULES=, and BGCOLOR=. For <TH> and <TD> tags, experiment more with the COLSPAN= and ROWSPAN= attributes more as well as with the NOWRAP option to see what it does to text.

TEST YOUR KNOWLEDGE

Create a staff directory table.

It should include centered horizontal table headings throughout the table that identify individual library departments.

Under each department and at the left side of the table, each staff member's name should be a table heading that takes up four rows vertically below, so you can include their: 1) job title, 2) mailing address, 3) phone number, 4) e-mail address each in separate cells below each other and to the right of the staff member's name.

Separate each department with one blank row before starting another department and list of names. Finally, add a bold caption to the top of the directory table.

5

Creating Frames

If you need assistance, see Chapter 2 for details on frame tags and attributes.

WHAT IS A FRAME?

Frames allow you to divide a Web page into a number of different windows. Each window is capable of displaying different content. It is possible to create any size or number of windows. Frames can both 1) let visitors look at more than one document at a time, and 2) let you control the manner in which information appears on the screen.

When you created your first Web site, you probably placed links to the rest of your Web site and any navigation buttons at the bottom of the page (see Figure 5–1, for example). This required a visitor to scroll through your entire document to reach help or navigate around your Web site. That design was, and still is, inefficient.

Frames enable you to provide visitors with navigation information that always displays. Visitors can easily move around your site and quickly reach different content sections or Web sites with a single click (see Figure 5–2, for example).

Hint: Frames allow visitors to view specific contents of your Web site while also providing them with a navigation tool.

GETTING FAMILIAR WITH FRAMES

Frames require you to think differently when planning and writing HTML documents. You will still write Web documents, such as pages discussing ILL, library policies and reference services, but you will also have to write an HTML document that describes how these pages will be displayed in the navigational frame, as well as a separate HTML document to set up the entire frame layout.

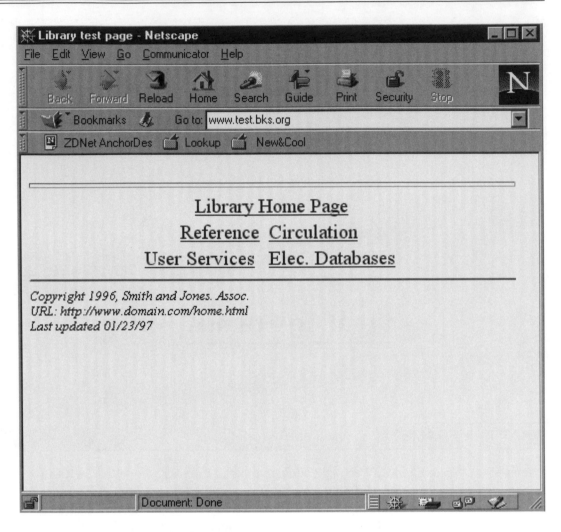

Figure 5–1: Non-Frame Web Page

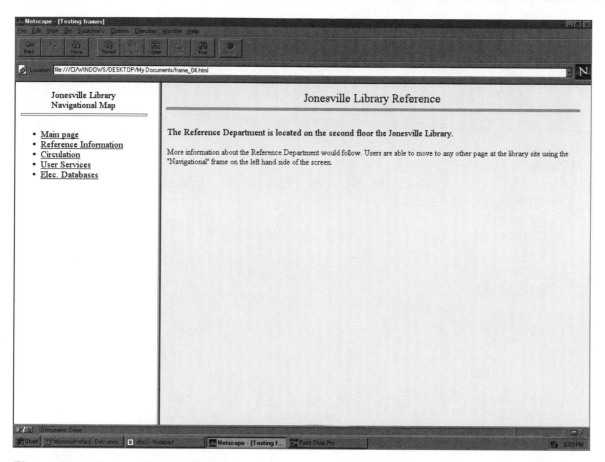

Figure 5–2: Frame-Based Web Page

To illustrate this concept see Figure 5–3, which is generated by three HTML documents. The main HTML document controls the layout of the frames on the screen, but does not itself contain any of the text displayed. The text that is displayed in both of the frames comes from two additional, and separate, HTML documents that are no different from any of the HTML documents you've already created.

> **Hint:** It's best to locate navigational frames on either the left-hand side of the screen, as in the illustration, or at the bottom of the screen. Navigational frames located at the top or right-hand side of a page often tend to confuse novice Web surfers.

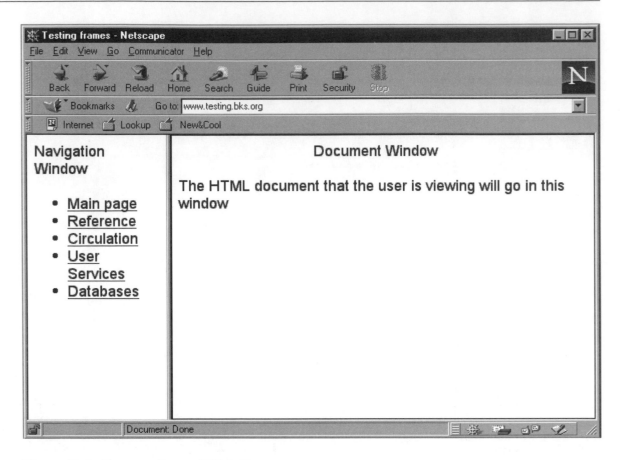

Figure 5–3: Frames-Based Web Page

STEP-BY-STEP INSTRUCTIONS FOR BUILDING A PAGE USING FRAMES

Creating a frames-based Web site will require you to learn a few new tags and forget some of the basic HTML rules you already probably know. You will be writing three HTML documents to create a single frame-based Web page, two HTML documents containing content, and one to determine the layout of the information to be presented. The layout HTML document is called the <FRAMESET> document.

First, let's talk about the "HTML basics" you will have to forget when creating frames. In non-frame HTML documents you are required to use the <BODY> tag. This tag cannot be used in a <FRAMESET> document. If you use a <BODY> tag the document will not display. Instead, you will use the <FRAMESET> tag in place of the <BODY> tag. It must appear in the same position in an HTML document as the <BODY> tag; before the first lines of text that will display, such as either an <H1> or <HR> tag. A good place to put the <FRAMESET> tag is right after the </HEAD> tag.

At this point your document will look like this:

```
<HTML>
<HEAD>
<TITLE>My Frames Page</TITLE>
</HEAD>
<FRAMESET>
```

STEP 1: DIVIDE THE PAGE

Let's look at the <FRAMESET> tag in a bit more detail. There are two significant pieces of information (attributes) that the <FRAMESET> tag can contain; COLS (columns) and ROWS. The COLS attribute is used to divide the document vertically, the ROWS attribute to divide the documents horizontally. These two attributes set up the size of the frame windows that will be displayed. You do not need to supply both, but you will need to specify a value for either COLS or ROWS to create a <FRAMESET> document that works as it should. There are two ways that you can specify a frame size. The first way is to specify the exact size in pixels; however, this is overly complex. The second, and easier, way to determine the size of a frame is to use percentages, separated by commas.

A page with two frames that divide the browser window vertically would have a <FRAMESET> tag like this:

<FRAMESET COLS=25%,75%>

If you want to add additional frame windows you would simply add another value to the list <FRAMESET COLS=20%,40%,40%>. In both cases it is important to not develop a page with column or row values that exceed 100 percent. If you do this the content of your document will not be displayed on the screen, but scroll either to the right or down.

Hint: You can specify "the rest of the value under 100%" by using an * in your frameset tag. <FRAMESET COLS=30%,40%,*> In this particular situation the * is equal to 30%; this value is relative to the other values in the frameset tag.

Borderless Frames

It is possible to create frames that have no visible borders. To do this add BORDER=0 to your <FRAMESET> tag. The resulting tag will look like this:

<FRAMESET COLS=25%,75% BORDER=0>

STEP 2: DEFINE THE DIFFERENT CONTENT FRAMES

Once you have determined how your page will be divided, you'll need to define the different content frames. The tag we'll start with is the <FRAME> tag. The <FRAME> tag is a single tag that doesn't require a </FRAME> tag to make it work correctly.

Attributes

There are attributes that need to be added to your <FRAME> tag. The first and most important of these attributes is SRC=. This attribute indicates the specific HTML docu-

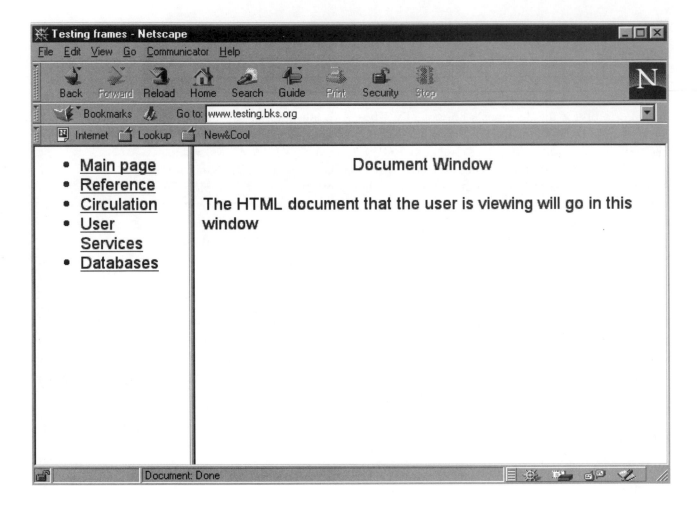

Figure 5–4: Different Frameset Arrangements

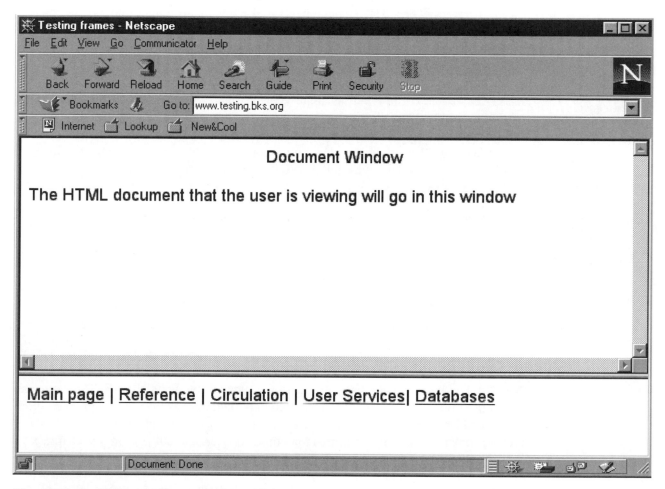

Figure 5–5: Different Frameset Arrangements

*This example is available
on the CD-ROM in the
HTML folder under:*
5–5.html

SRC=
"FILENAME.
HTML"—
determines the
source that will be
used to fill a frame.

ment that will fill the frame.

<FRAME SRC= "http://www.ohionet.org">

The HTML document identified in the SRC= attribute needs to be a separate HTML document. To begin, you might want to choose existing Web documents to be the source for your frames. These HTML documents will require only minor and simple changes in their HTML coding to make them function efficiently in the frames environment. We will discuss these changes after we finish discussing the other important attributes of the <FRAME> tag.

NORESIZE—
determines if the
user will be able to
resize a frame.

RESIZE. The next important attribute you must add to the <FRAME> tag has to do with resizability. This allows visitors to alter the dimensions of your frame windows. The default setting allows visitors to manually adjust the size of windows produced by your Web page. If you want to have total control over the presentation of your page you can change this default by adding NORESIZE to your frame tag.

At this point the frame tag will look like this:

<FRAME SRC ="http://www.ohionet.org" NORESIZE>

SCROLLING=
YES/NO/AUTO—
determines if the
user scrolls
through the frame
window.

SCROLLING. The SCROLLING attribute allows visitors to scroll down or across the windows of your frames-based page. The possible settings for this argument are YES, NO, or AUTO. If SCROLLING is set to YES for a window the scroll bars will appear at the right hand side or bottom of the frame.

The example below creates a frame with "as needed" scrolling.

<FRAME SRC="http://www.ohionet.org/" NORESIZE SCROLLING=AUTO>

NAME=
"FRAME_NAME"—
is name of the
frame. It will be
important when
using frame
targets.

NAME. The last attribute that you'll assign to your frame is its NAME. The name can be almost anything. You should follow three important rules: 1. the name should be short, 2. it should be case sensitive, and 3. there should be no spaces in the name as these create problems "targeting" frames (something you learn about later in this chapter).

The following example creates a frame named "content."

<FRAME SRC="http://www.ohionet.org/" NORESIZE SCROLLING=AUTO NAME="content">

DESIGN TIPS

Both of the examples above divide the screen into two windows. It is possible for you to divide the page even further, to display three, four, or more frames simultaneously. This is a case where more is not better. Creating a page that displays more than two frames is visually distracting to visitors. It's best to stick with just two frames per page, one for navigation and the other to display specific information.

STEP 3: GET FRAMES TO WORK TOGETHER

Targeting Frames

After you have set up the <FRAME> tag and selected the appropriate attributes, it's time to determine how the frames will function together. The frame example is structured so that when a visitor clicks on a link in the navigational frame, the HTML document you request will appear in that same window. This makes your navigational frame essentially useless, as it will disappear after just one click. To solve this problem you need to direct the navigational frame to "target" another frame. Once this is set up, when a link is selected the contents of the retrieved document displays in the other (or "targeted") frame. To set up frame targeting you will need to make a small change in each of the link tags in your standard HTML documents.

A normal link tag looks like this:

<A HREF="URL"> text**</A>**

To "frame target" a document, change your link to the format below:

<A HREF="URL" TARGET="TARGET_FRAME"> text**</A>**

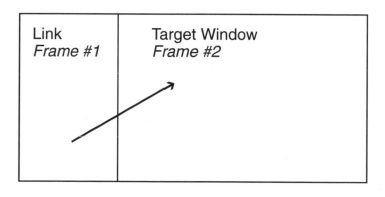

The example below creates three links that target a frame named "content":

<A HREF="main.html" TARGET="content">Main Page**</A>**
<A HREF="reference.html" TARGET="content">Reference Information**</A>**
<A HREF="comm_cal.html" TARGET="content">Community Calendar**</A>**

There are a number of additional options available when using frame targeting. The most useful of these is the ability to open a new browser window instead of targeting an existing frame. This can be confusing to novice Web surfers, who don't realize that they have opened another browser window. Therefore, think carefully before implementing this type of targeting. To setup "new window" targeting, see the example below to links that you want to open, in new windows

<A HREF="URL" TARGET="_BLANK" >

Hint: The presence of multiple scroll bars can be distracting for visitors; however, the only thing worse than too many visible scroll bars is not seeing a scroll bar when one is needed. Therefore, the best setting is AUTO. By using the AUTO setting, scrollbars will appear only if needed.

Hint: Remember without the use of the TARGET= attribute the document retrieved by the hypertext link would be displayed in the same frame as the link you clicked.

Hint: After reading about all of these attributes, frames may begin to seem unnecessarily complex, but they're really not. To create your first frame, just take it one step at a time. Use the handy checklist at the end of this chapter.

STEP 4: HELP VISITORS WHOSE BROWSERS DON'T SUPPORT FRAMES

There is only one more area of frames to explore—how to help visitors with browsers that don't display frames. Welcome to the world of "noframes." The <NOFRAMES> tag is important only if a visitor's browser does not support frames. The <NOFRAMES> tag will deliver an error message to such a visitor, informing them that they are trying to access a frames-based site with a browser that is not capable of viewing frames. You may also want to add links to access a non-frame version of your Web site or to allow visitors to download a frames-capable browser.

The <NOFRAMES> tag works in a manner similar to that of the <BODY> tag. Any text between the opening and closing </NOFRAMES> tags will be displayed, but only if visitors do not have a frames-capable browser.

NOFRAMES—Tag to be used on a frames-based Web page that supplies information to visitors without frames-capable browsers.

Hint: Be sure to include non-frame document links for visitors without frames-capable browsers. Failing to do so may create difficulties for up to 10 percent of visitors trying to view your Web site.

> *HTML Document With a <NOFRAMES> Error Message*
>
> ```
> <HTML>
> <HEAD>
> <TITLE>Testing Frames</TITLE>
> </HEAD>
> <FRAMESET COLS=75%,25%>
> <FRAME NAME="navigation" NORESIZE SCROLLING="YES"
> SRC="nav.html">
> <FRAME NAME="content" NORESIZE SCROLLING="YES"
> SRC="content.html">
> <!—Error message to non-frames capable browsers—>
> <NOFRAMES><FONT SIZE=4> Sorry this document must be viewed with
> a frames capable browser. Please go to the <A HREF="old_browser.html">
> non-frames</A> version of this page.
> </NOFRAMES>
> </FRAMESET>
> </HTML>
> ```

The above error message informs visitors that they cannot use the Web page as it was designed, but a version of the page, which does not contain frames, is available. Additionally it is useful to offer a link to a non-frame version of your Web site.

WHAT YOU'VE LEARNED SO FAR

1. Decide how many frames you want. Decide if you want them to be horizontal or vertical. Sketch the layout on paper.
2. Write HTML documents to be used as text inside the frames you create.
3. Begin to write your <FRAMESET> page.
4. Choose the attributes you'll use with each frame.
   SRC=
   NORESIZE
   SCROLLING=
   NAME=
5. Use <NOFRAMES> messages to inform visitors who do not have frames-capable browsers.

TEST YOUR KNOWLEDGE

Using the checklist above, create a frames-based Web page. It should contain the following elements:

- A navigational frame that allows visitors to easily access the major sections of your Web site. This frame should not allow scrolling. Try to fit all the navigational information into one screen. Remember that links in the navigational frame must target the document frame.
- A provision for visitors with non-frames browsers, so that they can be directed to a non-frames version of your site.
- A document frame that allows visitors to scroll, but not resize your frames.

6

Creating Forms

*If you need assistance, see **Chapter 2** for form tags and attributes.*

WHAT IS A FORM?

When designing a Web site it is necessary to begin with basic HTML, but to develop the best possible Web presence for your library, you'll need to begin learning skills other than HTML. In this chapter you'll begin by learning HTML tags to create interactive forms for visitors.

Forms allow visitors to interact with your Web site as well as to tailor their experience to their own needs. Your Web site won't just contain static information, but instead it will be transformed into an adaptable document that delivers dynamic information to better serve visitors.

The process of developing forms consists of two parts:

- Creating an HTML document/form that visitors will see when they view your Web site.
- Creating a script, or small program, that handles the information visitors submit via your HTML document/form.

This chapter will teach you the tags necessary to create an HTML form. Starting in Chapter 7 you will learn to create scripts to handle the information gathered by the forms that you create. It's necessary to learn both parts, if you are going to use forms on your Web site.

PLANNING A FORM

The first step to creating a Web form is to determine the type of services you would like to offer to visitors. The range of possible services is quite broad. Would you like to allow visitors to:

- Submit questions to your reference staff?
- Apply for a library card?
- Put a hold on reserve or charged materials?
- Search a local database your library has developed?

Hint: Remember there will probably not be any library staff members helping visitors complete the forms. Therefore, everything needs to be self-explanatory.

Next, you'll need to decide what information to include on, and get from, the form. You should complete these first two steps prior to writing any HTML forms. Once you know the type of information you'll need, think about how visitors will interact with the form. Is the form well organized and easily understood? You may even want to sketch your form prior to writing any HTML code.

If you are creating a Web-based form that is based on an already-existing paper form, resist the temptation to simply create an online version of it. Remember there are new issues to think about and design for. For instance: What will you do about a signature? How will transactions that require photo identification be handled? You may want to consider completely redesigning any forms you move to the Web.

TIPS TO REMEMBER

- It is not advisable, at this time, to obtain credit card numbers or other highly personal information through a Web form unless you are employing advanced encryption techniques such as SSL.
- Don't make forms too long. Visitors tend to have a very low tolerance for time-consuming tasks. They may not use the scroll bar to view your whole form. Long forms can also be very confusing for novice Web surfers.
- Be sure to test form instructions. Visitors should be able to quickly understand how to fill out any form.
- Design forms like you would any other Web document. Forms should display correctly on a standard 15" monitor with a resolution of 640 x 480.
- Remember that you will be working with both an HTML document and a script (program) on your Web server. Both of these parts must be present and work correctly with one another.

FORM TAG BASICS

The basic tag pair <FORM> </FORM> identifies text as part of a form. The <FORM> tag is the first tag in any form and the </FORM> tag is the last tag.

Inside the opening <FORM> tag include both the METHOD= and ACTION= attributes. The METHOD= attribute tells the visitor's browser how to send the form to your Web server. The ACTION= attribute points the visitor's browser to the script on your Web server so that it can process the form content.

<FORM METHOD="GET" ACTION ="http://198.30.145.82/cgi-bin/hi.pl**">**

The METHOD= attribute tells browsers how to send information back to your Web server. The two most popular options are GET and POST. Of the two options GET is preferred because it is compatible with more Web servers than POST. These options really aren't that different from one another and do basically the same thing; some servers though do not support the use of the GET option.

The next attribute to add to the form tag is ACTION=, which is the URL of the script to be run on your Web server. This script program, 99 percent of the time, will need to be located in a directory called CGI-BIN. To help preserve the security of your Web server, forms can access scripts only if they are in the CGI-BIN directory. To avoid possible confusion always be sure to specify a complete URL in your forms.

http://www.xyz.com/cgi-bin/file.pl

> The <FORM> tag has two attributes: ACTION= and METHOD=. METHOD= tells a browser how to send information to your Web server. ACTION= specifies the name/location of the script that will be used to process the data.

WHAT YOU'VE LEARNED SO FAR

- A form is an HTML document that can send information to your Web server.
- Form information is processed by a script on your Web server.
- Scripts can perform a number of functions including: reserving materials, fielding reference questions, and allowing visitors to search databases.
- All forms begin with a <FORM> tag that must have both an ACTION= and a METHOD= attribute.
- A normal opening form tag looks like this: <FORM METHOD="POST" ACTION="http://www.ohionet.org/cgi-bin/hello.pl">
- Because you are allowing a visitor to run a program on your computer, security should be a concern. We will be addressing this and other issues in Chapters 7, 8, and 9.
- You should now be ready to move on.

Hint: Be sure not to forget the closing </FORM> tag. If you do, you won't see any of your form when you try to view it.

FORM ELEMENTS: NAME AND TYPE

In addition to the <FORM> </FORM> tag pair, all forms have elements. Elements are the areas that allow visitors to enter information. In this part you will: 1) learn some of the basic types of form elements, and 2) learn how to create forms containing the different types of elements.

All elements in a form must contain two attributes, NAME= and TYPE=. In order to function properly all elements in your form must first have a name, so that your Web server knows how to refer to the information a visitor keys in. Without a name your form will not function correctly and the information entered will be discarded.

HOW DO YOU NAME ELEMENTS?

Each form element must have a unique name. How do you name the form elements? There are hundreds of different ways to name them. It's important to develop a naming system that you understand and use consistently throughout your Web site. For instance, if a form element asks for a first name I'll name the element "first_name" or if it asks for an address I'll call it simply "address."

NAMING TIPS

- There are no spaces or punctuation other than the underscore character (_) allowed in the NAME= attribute.
- Element names are case-sensitive. Develop your own consistent system for using capital and lowercase letters.
- Use simple names if possible. This will save time and, if problems develop, make them easier to fix.

TYPE BASICS

The next attribute of the <FORM> tag is TYPE=. Specifying the type of element determines how it will look and behave. Some form element types allow visitors to type information; others allow visitors to select from lists of items, or use checkboxes or radio buttons. Due to the wide variety of form type choices, it is necessary to specify a type for each individual form element. If you fail to specify a type for a form element, your form will not operate properly. The next section will examine the individual element types and their potential uses.

Enter your name

Figure 6–1: Single-Line Text Input Box

SINGLE-LINE TEXT INPUT BOXES

The form element we begin with, is also the simplest. It produces an input box that allows the visitors to enter a single line of text. These boxes are the most commonly used of all form elements.

When you create this box you will need to specify the following options:

- **INPUT TYPE=**—set to "TEXT."
- **SIZE=**—specified as a number of characters (SIZE=25 will create a box that will hold 25 characters and/or spaces).
- **NAME=**—the unique name of the form element.

The tagging will look like this:

<INPUT TYPE="TEXT" **NAME=**"NORMAL" **SIZE=25>**

This creates a box that holds up to 25 characters without scrolling. The box will appear to hold 25 characters, but it is able to handle much more text than that. If a visitor continues to type, text will scroll to the right.

Our example will now look like this:

<INPUT TYPE="TEXT" **NAME=**"NORMAL" **SIZE=25 MAXLENGTH=100>**

MULTIPLE-LINE TEXT INPUT BOXES

Enter your street address

Figure 6–2: Multiple-Line Text Input Box

Hint: This box can be used for information like names, dates, or other data that can be entered into a single line.

Hint: As a security precaution, specify the maximum length for the input box by using the MAXLENGTH= attribute. As a rule, the value of this attribute is usually set around 100.

An additional example can be found on the CD-ROM in the HTML folder under:
6–1.html

Hint: Use <TEXTAREA> to allow a visitor to provide an address, comments, thoughts, or ideas in paragraph format— essentially any data that requires room for multiple-line data entry

There will probably be some information that you would like a visitor to supply that will be longer than a single line in length. For situations where you need to allow visitors to enter multiple lines of text information, use the <TEXTAREA> tag. The basic format for this tag is:

<TEXTAREA> </TEXTAREA>

When you create a multiple-line text input box you will need to specify the following options:

- An opening <TEXTAREA> tag.
- The number of COLS (Columns) and ROWS.
- The name of your text area.
- Instructional text that will appear inside the box.
- A closing </TEXTAREA> tag.

Hint: Due to the varying types of information a visitor needs to key into an Inter-library loan form, they rarely include multiple choice elements, such as checkboxes or radio buttons. ILL forms use mostly text input boxes.

An example will look like this:

<TEXTAREA NAME="STREET_ADDRESS" **COLS=**40 **ROWS=**5>
Type your street address and seven digit zip code here
</TEXTAREA>

This tag will create a multiple-line input box that is named STREET_ADDRESS. It will have forty columns and five rows. This is determined by the attributes COLS=40 and ROWS=5. The text between the opening and closing of the <TEXTAREA> tags will appear in the box by default.

RADIO BUTTONS

View this file on CD-ROM in the HTML folder under: 6–2.html

Trivia: Why are they called radio buttons? Because they look like the buttons used on an old car radio to select stations.

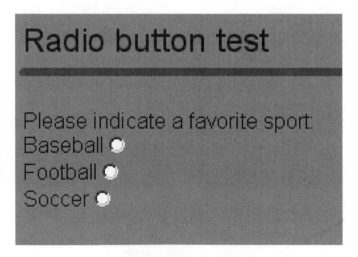

Figure 6–3: Radio Button

Not every form requires visitors to enter text. In some situations you'll want to provide visitors with multiple-choice response options. Using radio buttons allows you to build a multiple-choice form.

When you create radio button form elements you'll need to specify the following options:

Hint: This element is a popular form element for YES/ NO or multiple-choice responses.

- **INPUT TYPE=**—in this case "RADIO" (a shortened form of radio button)
- **NAME=**—all answer choices for the same question should share the same name.
- **VALUE=**—for the element.

This is the first time that you've had to specify a VALUE= attribute for a form element. Because visitors will not be entering a text answer you will need to associate a different value with each radio form element. Values can be anything from numbers to words (like yes, no, and maybe) or phrases.

In the following example, if a visitor clicks the first radio button the value of the ADULT_CARD element sent to your server will be NO. If they click the second button the value sent will be YES.

Hint: Remember that each set of radio buttons must have a unique name. Each button should also have a different value. No, and Yes.

```
<INPUT TYPE="RADIO" NAME="ADULT_CARD" VALUE="NO">
<INPUT TYPE="RADIO" NAME="ADULT_CARD" VALUE="YES">
```

Radio buttons have one disadvantage—they require visitors to select an option. For responses to questions that are optional, you may want to use a checkbox.

CHECKBOXES

*A working version of the above example is found on the CD-ROM in the HTML folder under: **6–3.html***

Please mark all services you use
on a regular basis

☐ Story Hour

☐ Inter-Library Loan

☐ Adult Reading Tutors

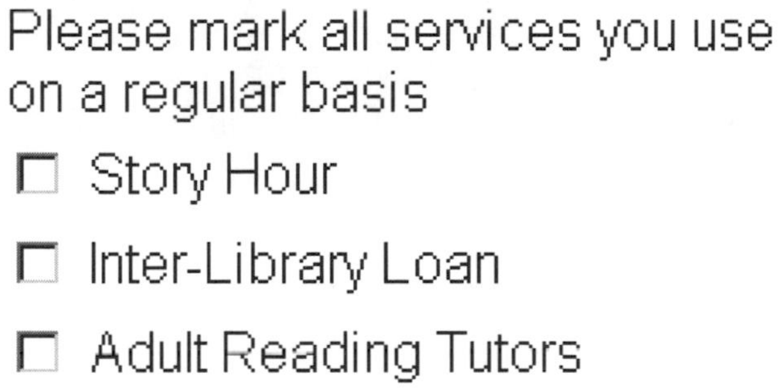

Figure 6–4: Checkbox

The CHECKBOX form element produces a small square box that a visitor can select by clicking in it. They are very similar to radio buttons, but are usually preferred in situations where an answer is optional.

When you create a checkbox you will need to specify the following tag options:

Hint: Use checkboxes in a library setting to do a survey.

A working example is found on the CD-ROM in the HTML folder under: 6–4.html

- **INPUT TYPE=**—set to CHECKBOX.
- **NAME=**—of the form element.
- **A VALUE=**—attribute for the form element.

A sample survey of library services:

Please mark all services you use on a regular basis:
Story Hour
<INPUT TYPE ="CHECKBOX" **NAME** ="STORY_HOUR" **VALUE**="ON">
Story Hour
<INPUT TYPE ="CHECKBOX" **NAME** ="ILL" **VALUE**="ON">ILL
<INPUT TYPE ="CHECKBOX" **NAME** ="ADULT_READING" **VALUE**="ON">
Adult Reading Tutors

PULL-DOWN LISTS

The SELECT element creates a "pull-down" menu that presents visitors with a number of predefined choices that visitors can select from. Each pull-down option is identified by a separate <OPTION> tag.

Please select your library type: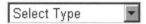

Figure 6–5: Select Pull-Down List

The SELECT form element allows you to create pull-down lists from which visitors are able to choose one option. This is one of the most professional-looking form elements and it is not difficult to create. Pull-down lists work well when information needs to be entered a very specific way. Advantages: 1) You will not have to deal with typing mistakes, 2) Visitors will be able to determine the form of information you need, 3) Pull-down lists take up only a small amount of space on a screen. They occupy as few as two lines, while providing visitors with long lists of choices that would be too big to display any other way. The format for the tag is: <SELECT> </SELECT>

When you create a pull-down list, you will need to specify the following tags and attributes:

- **NAME=**—the unique name for the form element
- **<OPTION> tags**—these will be the choices in the pull-down list:

Hint: When creating a list of pull-down items, be sure to organize them either alphabetically or in some other meaningful manner.

<SELECT NAME="LIBRARY_TYPE**">**
<OPTION>Academic (Large)
<OPTION>Academic (Small)
<OPTION>Public (Large)
<OPTION>Public (Small)
<OPTION>Special (Large)
<OPTION>Special (Small)
</SELECT>

In the sample list above, the first item that appears in the SELECT box will be Academic (Large). If you add an additional line of code <OPTION VALUE=" ">Select Type to the top of the list, when a visitor loads the page they will first see "Select Type" above all the checkbox options. This option provides visitors with instructions and/or explanations when using a pull-down list.

The coding for the pull-down list now looks like this:

```
<SELECT NAME="LIBRARY_TYPE">
<OPTION VALUE=" ">Select Type
<OPTION>Academic (Large)
<OPTION>Academic (Small)
<OPTION>Public (Large)
<OPTION>Public (Small)
<OPTION>Special (Large)
<OPTION>Special (Small)
</SELECT>
```

A working example of this pull-down list is included on the CD-ROM in the HTML folder under: 6–5.html

PASSWORD

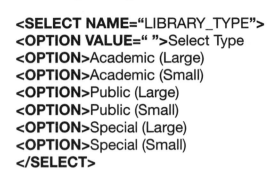

Figure 6–6: Password Text Box

A PASSWORD form type element looks similar to a single-line text entry box until a visitor begins to type. Then, instead of text, all a visitor will see is *****. When you create a PASSWORD element you will need to specify the following tag attributes:

- **INPUT TYPE=**—set to PASSWORD
- **NAME=**—the unique name for each form element

When combined, the coding for a password text box will look like this:

```
<INPUT TYPE="PASSWORD" NAME="USER_PASS">
```

Using this form type element does not mean that the text typed into it is encrypted or safe in any way. Passworded text, while not displayed on a visitors screen, will be sent to your Web server as plain text, which can easily be intercepted and compromised.

HIDDEN FORM ELEMENTS

One of the most advanced form elements you can use is the HIDDEN form type element, which allows you to pass along information with the form that a visitor will not see. Hidden elements are used mostly in interactive forms, which will be discussed in Chapters 8 and 9.

Hint: Creating a hidden form element is much easier than understanding why you might ever need to use this option. But trust us, as you become more advanced in the creation of Web-based forms you will frequently turn to this element.

Why might you want to create form with hidden data? Suppose that you want the form a visitor completes to generate data such as the visitor's name. You don't want to display this data to your visitor, but do need to access it with another program or display it in another Web page. You could use a hidden form element to pass this information to other forms or Web pages. This will allow your pages and programs to "remember" specific information.

When you create a hidden form element you will need to specify the following options:

• **INPUT TYPE=**—set to HIDDEN.
• **NAME=**—for each element.
• **VALUE=**—the hidden information to be passed along.

When combined, the example looks like this:

<INPUT TYPE="HIDDEN" **NAME=**"NAME" **VALUE=**"JOE SMITH">

ACTION BUTTONS

All of the form elements that we have examined so far are useful. But there is something missing: a way to get the information to the Web server. Up to this point you have created an HTML form containing various elements that can hold data but so far there is no way to send that data to your Web server. The final part of the form creation process is to add action buttons that allow you to send the form's information to your Web server for processing. There are two popular button types: SUBMIT and RESET.

SUBMIT BUTTONS

Figure 6–7: Submit Button

When clicked on, the submit button sends the information contained in your form elements to your Web server. Without this button, the information on your form will not be sent to your server.

When you create a submit button you will need to specify the following tag options:
• **INPUT TYPE=**—set to SUBMIT.
• **VALUE=**—Will appear as text on the face of the button. Most sites use either SUBMIT or SEND as the values.

When combined, the example will look like this:

<INPUT TYPE="SUBMIT" **VALUE=**"SUBMIT">

You might have noticed that there is no name attribute for a submit button. Due to the role this element plays there is no need to provide a name.

RESET BUTTONS

Figure 6–8: Reset Button

A reset button is designed to tell a visitor's browser to reset all your form's fields back to their original values. It is common to include such a button in the forms that you create, in order to allow visitors to quickly correct mistakes they may have made filling out a form.

When you create a reset button you will need to specify the following tag options:

- **INPUT TYPE=**—set to RESET.
- **VALUE=**—This text will appear on the face of the button. Most sites use either CLEAR or RESET as the values.

When combined, the example will look like this:

<INPUT TYPE="RESET" VALUE="RESET">

Just like the submit button there is no need to provide a name.

WHAT YOU'VE LEARNED SO FAR

These are all the new HTML tags and attributes you need to know to create usable forms. You have learned all about the <FORM> tag and various other tags, attributes, and options. If you do not feel comfortable with what you've learned so far, take some time to reread and learn them before moving on to the next chapter. Chapter 7 will provide you with working library form examples that will illustrate how you can use all of the tags, attributes, and options you've just learned to create a Web site that will really impress—and better serve—your users.

7

HTML Forms You Can Use

This chapter provides the HTML coding for a number of sample forms that you can modify to build your own Web forms: Interlibrary Loan (ILL) Request Form, Materials Reserve/Hold Form, Library Card Application Form, and Material Purchase Request Form. Pay particular attention to the layout of each Web document and how the form elements are structured. Remember that the coding in this section is just the first part of making a form work. In Chapter 8 you'll begin to learn how to create a program/ script to process form information.

TIPS FOR CREATING BETTER FORMS

- Use tables if possible. Tables allow all of the elements of the form to line up, and create a very professional appearing page.
- Don't forget about visitor security. Don't ask for sensitive or confidential information.
- Develop forms that minimize scrolling.
- Provide clear instructions for filling out forms.

A working version of this form can be found on the CD-ROM in the HTML folder under:
7–1.html

INTERLIBRARY LOAN REQUEST FORM

This sample form allows visitors to submit an interlibrary loan request via the Web.

Interlibrary Loan request form

Please complete all fields in this form and click the "Submit Information" button to request Interlibrary Loan materials.

Item Information

Name of item:

Author:

Date of Publication

Pages Needed:

Patron Information

Patron Name:

Library Card Number:

Phone Number:

E-mail address:

Date item is no longer needed:

| Submit Information | Clear Information |

Figure 7–1: Sample ILL Form

```
<HTML>
<HEAD>
<TITLE>ILL Form</TITLE>
</HEAD>
<BODY BGCOLOR="CAAAAC">
<FONT SIZE=6>
<I>Interlibrary Loan request form</I>
</FONT>
<HR SIZE=6 NOSHADE><FONT SIZE=4>
```
Please complete all fields in this form and click the "Submit Information" button to request materials through Interlibrary Loan.
```
<FORM ACTION="http://www.yourserver.com" METHOD="GET">
<TABLE CELLPADDING=6>
<TR><TD COLSPAN=4><FONT SIZE=5><I>Item Information</I>
<HR>
<TR><TD><FONT SIZE=4>Name of item:
<TD> <INPUT TYPE="TEXT" NAME="ITEM" SIZE=50>
<TR><TD><FONT SIZE=4>Author:
<TD><INPUT TYPE="TEXT" NAME="AUTHOR" SIZE=40>
<TR><TD><FONT SIZE=4>Date of Publication:
<TD><INPUT TYPE="TEXT" NAME="DATE_OF_PUB">
<TR><TD><FONT SIZE=4>Pages Needed:
<TD><INPUT TYPE="TEXT" NAME="PAGES">
<TR><TD COLSPAN=4><FONT SIZE=5><I>Patron Information</I>
<HR>
<TR><TD><FONT SIZE=4>Patron Name:
<TD><INPUT TYPE="TEXT" NAME="USER_NAME" SIZE=30>
<TR><TD><FONT SIZE=4>Library Card Number:
<TD><INPUT TYPE="TEXT" NAME="CARD_NUMBER" SIZE=15>
<TR><TD><FONT SIZE=4>Phone Number:
<TD><INPUT TYPE="TEXT" NAME="PHONE" SIZE=15>
<TR><TD><FONT SIZE=4>E-mail address:
<TD><INPUT TYPE="TEXT" NAME="EMAIL">
<TR><TD><FONT SIZE=4>Date item is no longer needed:
<TD><INPUT TYPE="TEXT" NAME="NEED_DATE">
</TABLE>
<INPUT TYPE="SUBMIT" VALUE="SUBMIT INFORMATION">
<INPUT TYPE="RESET" VALUE="CLEAR INFORMATION">
</FORM>
</BODY>
</HTML>
```

This example shows an abbreviated form of coding in which the table tags are not expressed as tag pairs. This coding not only works, but can save you lots of additional typing.

A working version of this form can be found on the CD-ROM in the HTML folder under:
7–2.html

MATERIALS RESERVE/HOLD FORM

This sample form allows patrons to put holds on library materials.

Materials Reservation Form

Please complete this form and click submit to place an item on reserve. The library will contact you when the materials are available for you to check out.

Call Number: [   ]

Title: [   ]

Author: [   ]

Type of material: [Select Material ▼]

Date Needed: [   ]

Your name: [   ]

Please contact me by: E-mail ○ Phone ○ Postcard ○

Contact Information: [   ]

[PLACE RESERVE]   [CLEAR FORM]

Figure 7–2: Materials Reserve/Hold Form

```
<HTML>
<HEAD>
<TITLE>Materials Reservation Form</TITLE>
</HEAD>
<BODY BGCOLOR="CAAAAC">
<FONT SIZE=6><CENTER>
Materials Reservation Form</FONT>
<HR SIZE=6 NOSHADE>
</CENTER>
```
Please complete this form and click submit to place an item on reserve. The library will contact you when the materials are available for you to check out.
```
<FORM ACTION="http://www.yourserver.com/cgi-bin/reserve.pl" METHOD="GET">
<TABLE>
<TR><TD><FONT SIZE=4>Call Number:
<TD><INPUT TYPE="TEXT" NAME="CALL_NUMBER" SIZE=35>
<TR><TD><FONT SIZE=4>Title:
<TD><INPUT TYPE="TEXT" NAME="TITLE" SIZE=50>
<TR><TD><FONT SIZE=4>Author:
<TD><INPUT TYPE="TEXT" NAME="AUTHOR" SIZE=35>
<TR><TD><FONT SIZE=4>Type of material:
<TD><SELECT NAME="MATERIAL_TYPE">
    <OPTION VALUE="">Select Material
    <OPTION>Hardback Book
    <OPTION>Paperback Book
    <OPTION>Audio Book
    <OPTION>Video
    <OPTION>CD (Music)
    <OPTION>CD (Data)
    <OPTION>Periodical
    </SELECT>
<TR><TD><FONT SIZE=4>Date Needed:
<TD><INPUT TYPE="TEXT" NAME="DATE">
<TR><TD><FONT SIZE=4>Your name:
<TD><INPUT TYPE="TEXT" NAME="USER_NAME" SIZE=50>
<TR><TD><FONT SIZE=4>Please contact me by:
<TD>
E-mail <INPUT TYPE="RADIO" NAME="CONTACT" VALUE="EMAIL">
Phone <INPUT TYPE="RADIO" NAME="CONTACT" VALUE="PHONE">
Postcard<INPUT TYPE="RADIO" NAME="CONTACT" VALUE="POST">
<TR><TD><FONT SIZE=4>Contact Information:
<TD><TEXTAREA NAME="CON_INFO" COLS=40 ROWS=3></TEXTAREA>
</TABLE>
<INPUT TYPE="SUBMIT" VALUE="PLACE RESERVE">
<INPUT TYPE="RESET" VALUE="CLEAR FORM">
</FORM>
</BODY>
</HTML>
```

This example shows an abbreviated form of coding in which the table tags are not expressed as tag pairs. By using this coding, which works, you will save yourself lots of additional typing.

A working version of this form can be found on the CD-ROM in the HTML folder under: 7–3.html

LIBRARY CARD APPLICATION FORM

This sample form allows patrons to apply for a library card via the Web. Some of the information can be set up as pre-defined responses so that you can use form elements such as radio buttons and select menus. Since this is a library card application, some of the information that you will need to gather to complete this application may be more private than the information previous forms have collected.

Library Card Application

Applying for a library card is easy using the Web. Just follow the simple steps below:

- *Complete all sections of this application form.*
- *Verify that all information is correct before clicking the "Submit" button.*
- *Click the "Submit" button.*
- *You can pick up your library card in three working days*

Please note:

You can pick up your new library card at the main branch information desk during normal hours. You will be required to present a photo ID.

Is this a new card, renewal, or replacement:	New ○ Renewal ○ Replacement ○
Last name:	[ ]
First name:	[ ]
Address:	[ ]
County of Residence:	[ ]
Phone:	[ ]
E-mail:	[ ]
Perfered contact:	E-mail ○ Phone ○ Postcard ○
Employer: (OPTIONAL)	[ ]
Work Phone: (OPTIONAL)	[ ]

I agree to comply with my library's policies and regulations. I agree to abide by the borrowing policies established by the Library Board of Trustees. I agree to replace or pay for the repair of all materials which are damaged while charged out to my card. I understand that violation of these polices can result in cancellation of my library privileges.

Clicking the apply button below signifies your agreement to the above. All information you supply is confidential and subject to verification.

[APPLY] [CLEAR FORM]

Figure 7–3: Library Card Application Form

```
<HTML>
<HEAD>
<TITLE> Library Card Application Form</TITLE>
</HEAD>
<BODY BGCOLOR="CAAAAC">
<FONT SIZE=6><CENTER>
Library Card Application</FONT>
<HR SIZE=6 NOSHADE>
<FORM ACTION="http://www.yourserver.com/cgi-bin/reserve.pl" METHOD="GET">
<TABLE BORDER=2>
<TR><TD COLSPAN=2>Applying for a library card is easy using the Web. Just follow the simple steps below:
<UL><I>
        <LI>Complete all sections of this application form.
        <LI>Verify that all information is correct before clicking the "Submit" button.
        <LI>Click the "Submit" button.
        <LI>You can pick up your library card in three working days
</I></UL>
<B>Please note:<P></B>
You can pick up your new library card at the main branch information desk during normal hours.
<BR>You will be required to present a photo ID.
<P>
<TR><TD><FONT SIZE=4>Is this a new card, renewal, or replacement: <TD>
New<INPUT TYPE="RADIO" NAME="C_TYPE" VALUE="NEW">
Renewal<INPUT TYPE="RADIO" NAME="C_TYPE" VALUE="RENEWAL">
Replacement<INPUT TYPE="RADIO" NAME="C_TYPE" VALUE="REPLACEMENT">
<TR><TD><FONT SIZE=4>Last name: <TD><INPUT TYPE="TEXT" NAME="LNAME" SIZE=30>
<TR><TD><FONT SIZE=4>First name:<TD><INPUT TYPE="TEXT" NAME="FNAME">
<TR><TD><FONT SIZE=4>Address:<TD><TEXTAREA NAME="ADDRESS" COLS=40 ROWS=3></TEXTAREA>
<TR><TD><FONT SIZE=4>County of Residence:<TD><INPUT TYPE="TEXT" NAME="COUNTY">
<TR><TD><FONT SIZE=4>Phone:<TD><INPUT TYPE="TEXT" NAME="PHONE">
<TR><TD><FONT SIZE=4>Email:<TD><INPUT TYPE="TEXT" NAME="EMAIL">
<TR><TD><FONT SIZE=4>Preferred contact: <TD>
E-mail <INPUT TYPE="RADIO" NAME="CONTACT" VALUE="EMAIL">
Phone <INPUT TYPE="RADIO" NAME="CONTACT" VALUE="PHONE">
Postcard<INPUT TYPE="RADIO" NAME="CONTACT" VALUE="POST">
<TR><TD><FONT SIZE=4>Employer:</B>(OPTIONAL)<TD><INPUT TYPE="TEXT" NAME="EMPLOY" SIZE=30>
<TR><TD><FONT SIZE=4>Work Phone:</B>(OPTIONAL)<TD><INPUT TYPE="TEXT" NAME="WK_PHONE">
</TABLE></CENTER>
<HR SIZE=6 NOSHADE>
<FONT SIZE=4>
I agree to comply with my library's policies and regulations. I agree to abide by the borrowing policies established by
the Library Board of Trustees. I agree to replace or pay for the repair of all materials which are damaged while charged
out to my card. I understand that violation of these polices can result in cancellation of my library privileges.
<P>
Clicking the apply button below signifies your agreement to the above. All information you supply is confidential and
subject to verification.
</FONT>
<P>
<INPUT TYPE="SUBMIT" VALUE="APPLY">
<INPUT TYPE="RESET" VALUE="CLEAR FORM">
</FORM>
</BODY>
</HTML>
```

This example shows an abbreviated form of coding in which the table tags are not expressed as tag pairs. You will save yourself lots of typing by using this type of coding.

A working version of this form can be found on the CD-ROM in the HTML folder under:
7–4.html

MATERIAL PURCHASE REQUEST FORM

This sample form allows patrons to submit suggestions to library staff for purchasing materials.

Material purchase request

To request that the library purchase materials:

- *Please complete as much of the following form as possible.*
- *If you need assistance please <u>contact</u> library support.*

Title: [   ]

Author: [   ]

Publisher: [   ]

Subject areas: [   ]

Your name: [   ]

Status: [Select Status ▼]

Your E-mail: [   ]

Your Library Card # : [   ]

[Submit Request] [Clear]

Figure 7–4: Material Purchase Request Form

```
<HTML>
<HEAD>
<TITLE>Material Purchase Request</TITLE>
</HEAD>
<BODY BGCOLOR="FFFFFF">
<CENTER><FONT SIZE=5>Material Purchase Request</FONT></CENTER>
<HR SIZE=6 NOSHADE>
<FONT SIZE=4>To request that the library purchase materials:
<UL><I>
<LI>Please complete as much of the following form as possible.
<LI>If you need assistance please
<A HREF="mail to: brad@library.lib.us">contact </A>library support.
</I></UL>
<TABLE>
<FORM ACTION="http://www.yourserver.com/cgi-bin/request.pl" METHOD="GET">
<TR><TD><FONT SIZE=4>Title:
<TD><INPUT TYPE="TEXT" NAME="TITLE" SIZE=40><TR><TD><FONT SIZE=4>Author:
<TD><INPUT TYPE="TEXT" NAME="AUTHOR" SIZE=40>
<TR><TD><FONT SIZE=4>Publisher:
<TD><INPUT TYPE="TEXT" NAME="PUB" SIZE=40>
<TR><TD><FONT SIZE=4>Subject areas:
<TD><INPUT TYPE="TEXT" NAME ="SUBS" SIZE=60>
<TR><TD><FONT SIZE=4>Your name:
<TD><INPUT TYPE="TEXT" NAME ="USER" SIZE=40>
<TR><TD><FONT SIZE=4>Status:<TD><SELECT NAME="STATUS">
<OPTION VALUE=""> Select Status
<OPTION>Faculty
<OPTION>Staff
<OPTION>Graduate
<OPTION>Undergraduate
</SELECT>
<TR><TD><FONT SIZE=4>Your Email:
<TD><INPUT TYPE="TEXT" NAME="USER_EMAIL" SIZE=40>
<TR><TD><FONT SIZE=4>Your Library Card #:
<TD><INPUT TYPE="TEXT" NAME="LIB_NUM" SIZE=10>
</TABLE>
<P>
<INPUT TYPE="SUBMIT" VALUE="SUBMIT REQUEST">
<INPUT TYPE="RESET" VALUE="CLEAR">
</FORM>
</BODY>
</HTML>
```

This example shows an abbreviated form of coding in which the table tags are not expressed as tag pairs. This coding works and can save you lots of additional typing.

WHAT YOU'VE LEARNED SO FAR

This chapter reviewed the HTML coding used to create forms. The four sample forms illustrate ways to use different form elements. Before continuing on to the next chapter be sure that you understand all of the HTML tags that are involved in creating an HTML form. Chapter 8 will focus on the "other side" of form creation—programming.

TEST YOUR KNOWLEDGE

1. Create a staff bibliographic record change request form using: three text-entry boxes, a checkbox, and a select list.

2. There are two errors in the code below. Can you locate them?

```
<FORM ACTION="http://www.yourserver.com">
Name: <INPUT TYPE="TEXT" SIZE=20>
Gender:
Male <INPUT TYPE="RADIO" VALUE="MALE" NAME="GENDER">
Female <INPUT TYPE="RADIO" VALUE="FEMALE" NAME="GENDER">
Would you like to be on our mailing list?:
<INPUT TYPE="CHECKBOX" NAME="MAIL">
</FORM>
```

Answers

- There is no METHOD= argument in the <FORM> tag.
- The CHECKBOX does not have a VALUE=ON argument.

8

PERL and CGI Basics

By now you should have a pretty good knowledge of HTML code. However, if you only use HTML, you can't provide visitors with the interactive experiences that a successful Web site needs. To add an interactive dimension to your Web site, you'll need to learn a programming language called *PERL* (Practical Extraction and Reporting Language).

You will be using PERL to write short programs, called *CGI scripts*, to handle the data from HTML forms. To learn PERL programming it's not necessary to learn every PERL command. These next two chapters will focus on the PERL commands and functions that you'll need to write CGI scripts to process Web-based forms.

Common Gateway Interface
acceptData, ProcessData, Return ...

GETTING STARTED WITH PERL

In order to use PERL to develop CGI scripts, you'll first have to install a PERL interpreter on your Web server. This may sound like a daunting task, but it really is not all that difficult.

If you will be using an operating system not listed above, connect to *http://www.perl.org* and download an appropriate version of the PERL interpreter software.

PERL BASICS: A FIRST PEEK

Look at page 104 for a glimpse of your first few lines of PERL programming. PERL will look somewhat intimidating at first, just like HTML did the first time that you saw it. Don't worry, though. PERL is not nearly as difficult as it appears at first glance. The section of PERL code that we will be working with is a header that you will place at the beginning of every PERL program you create.

*There are copies of the PERL interpreter and installation instructions included on the CD-ROM in the Programs folder. Install **win-perl** if using the Windows NT, Windows 95/98/NT operating system. Install **unix-perl** if using the Linux or UNIX operating systems.*

HOW DO YOU KNOW IF YOU ALREADY HAVE A
PERL INTERPRETER INSTALLED ON YOUR WEB SERVER?

Depending on the type of Web server you are using, follow the instructions below to see if a PERL interpreter is already installed on your server:

- **Linux**—Type <u>which PERL</u>. This will tell you where the interpreter is and what version of PERL is installed.
- **UNIX**—Type <u>which PERL</u>. This will tell you where the interpreter is and what version of PERL is installed.
- **Windows 95/Windows NT**—open a command prompt and type <u>dir /s perl.exe</u>.

If an interpreter is already installed on your server, there is no need to install one from the CD-ROM.

BEGINNING PERL TIPS

- Do not test PERL programs you are writing on "live" HTML pages (pages accessible to anyone on the Web). Instead develop an internal test area on your Web server. Be sure to test all new PERL programs under a variety of different conditions before putting them up live on the Web.
- Design PERL programs that emphasize security. This will not only protect you from hackers but also from inadvertent mistakes made by visitors.
- There is no one "right" or "wrong" way to develop programs in PERL. Feel free to experiment with different programming styles.
- PERL programs are case-sensitive.
- PERL code must be created with a text editing program that can output ASCII text. Most word processing programs—even the simple Windows/NT Notepad and Wordpad programs—can do this.
- All PERL program files must have a file extension of .pl.

---

*This code is contained in a file on the CD-ROM in the scripts folder under: **cgi-lib.pl**. This file should be copied from the CD-ROM to the CGI-BIN directory of your Web server.*

```
#! usr/bin/perl
push(@INC,"/usr/WWW/httpd/public/cgi-bin");
require ("cgi-lib.pl");
&ReadParse;
print &PrintHeader;
```

The above five lines may look confusing, but we'll explain it line by line.

- The first line *#! usr/bin/perl* is a path statement that tells the program where the PERL interpreter is located. Once you figure out the location of the PERL interpreter on your Web server, modify this line of code so that it specifies that location. This line will remain the same in all your programs. It will always start with *#!* and then the path (directory) will follow. All PERL scripts must start with this line of code.

- The second line *push(@INC, "/usr/WWW/httpd/public/cgi-bin");* tells the program the location of your Web server's CGI-BIN directory. If you have not created such a directory, now is the time to do that. Consult the documentation that accompanies your Web server software to learn more about setting up a CGI-BIN directory (or have your "techie" do this for you). You will want to save all of your PERL scripts in the CGI-BIN directory. This line will always start with *push(@INC,* put the path to your CGI-BIN directory after the comma and then add *");* to end the line.
- The third line *require ("cgi-lib.pl");* tells the PERL program to use a special set of pre-written PERL code. This pre-written code is designed to help users create CGI-BIN programs in PERL by automating a number of difficult functions.
- The fourth and fifth lines *&ReadParse;* and *print &PrintHeader;* tells the PERL program to use some of the pre-written coding found in the cgi-lib.pl file. Specifically, the first command tells your PERL program how to handle the data being submitted from your HTML form while the second command tells your program how to send a response back to the visitor filling out your form.

Note that most of the lines in the sample end with a semicolon. This is true for most lines of PERL code. The only line we've dealt with so far that doesn't end with a semicolon is the first line. You will notice later that there are a few more lines of coding where semicolons are not needed, but I'll explain them as we explore more of PERL. For now, assume that you will need to end lines with the semicolon.

Congratulations! You made it though your first few lines of PERL. The good news is that you can copy the header that we just explored directly into your first PERL script. The only text that you will need to change will be the path statements in the first and second lines.

YOUR FIRST PERL PROGRAM

THE *PRINT* FUNCTION

Every program that you create for your Web site will need to display information. This can be accomplished in PERL by using the print function to display information on a visitor's computer screen, in an e-mail message, or into a file. The default setting for the print function is to print information to the visitor's screen. Let's look at that first. The syntax is simple:

print (" ");

Just fill in the area between the quotation marks with what you want to display on the computer screen.

This line of code displays the words "Hello world" on the screen:

print ("Hello world");

WINDOWS NT USERS

You may experience difficulty with the previous header format. If you are using a Windows NT Server use the following header instead.

```
#!c:\netscape\perl\perl5\perl.exe
print "HTTP/1.0 200 OK";
print "Content-type: text/html \n\n";
push(@INC,"c:\netscape\server\docs\register\cgi-bin");

$in= $ENV{'QUERY_STRING'};
@in= split(/[&;]/,$in);
foreach $i (0 .. $#in) {

# Convert plus's to spaces
$in[$i] =~ s/\+/ /g;
# Split into key and value.
($key, $val)= split(/=/,$in[$i],2); # splits on the first =.

# Convert %XX from hex numbers to alphanumeric
$key =~ s/%(..)/pack("c",hex($1))/ge;
$val =~ s/%(..)/pack("c",hex($1))/ge;

# Associate key and value
$in{$key} .= "\0" if (defined($in{$key})); # \0 is the multiple separator
$in{$key} .= $val;
}
```

This header can be copied into your PERL scripts, running on Windows NT servers, with only two modifications. The first line *#!c:\netscape\perl\perl5\perl.exe,* the path that tells the program where the PERL interpreter is located, must be changed so that it specifies the location of the PERL interpreter on your NT server. The second modification you need to make is in the fourth line *push(@INC,"c:\ netscape\server\docs\register\cgi-bin");* this line tells your program the location of your server's CGI-BIN directory. If you have not made one yet now is the time to do that. Consult the documentation that accompanied your NT server software to learn more about setting up a CGI-BIN directory.

Likewise, the following line of code will display "1 2 3" on the screen

```
print ("1 2 3");
```

Below is a PERL program that will actually run using what we have learned so far. It will print the words "Hello World" on the screen. Remember you may have to change the path statements in the first and second lines of code to make it run on your computer (see the last bullet on page 104 and the first bullet on page 105).

```
#! usr/bin/perl
push(@INC,"/data1/ip/iubks/cgi-bin/");
require ("cgi-lib.pl");
&ReadParse;
print &PrintHeader;
## End of the header ##—- This is a comment line.
print ("Hello World");
```

You will use the print function frequently when creating programs to process the forms for your Web site. This function will allow your PERL script to communicate with visitors to your form and provide them with feedback.

The previous program runs, but what you see is not too exciting, so let's spice it up a bit.

```
#! usr/local/bin/perl
push(@INC,"/data1/ip/iubks/cgi-bin/");
require ("cgi-lib.pl");
&ReadParse;
print &PrintHeader;
print ("<html><head><title>Hello World</title></head>");
print ("<body bgcolor=\"ffffff\"> <font size=6><blink> Hello");
print ("World</blink><p></html>");
```

This script will produce a blinking Hello World statement on a white background. As you look at the PERL code above, notice the HTML tags in the print statements. One of the biggest challenges that you will face when creating PERL scripts is thinking and writing in two languages: PERL and HTML. You will have to do this to be a successful CGI programmer. The HTML coding in the above example is slightly different than normal HTML. Notice the presence of the \ character prior to the quotation marks in the <body bgcolor=\"ffffff\"> tag. The \ character is called an *escape character*. PERL gives some characters special meaning ($, " , ( ) , @ , % , \). If you want to print these characters on a visitor's computer screen, you must precede them with a \ character. The escape character tells the computer that you don't want the character to retain its special meaning, you just want it to be displayed on the screen. (This is similar to the HTML equivalent characters < > & ; .)

The PERL coding to display the phrase "You receive a 95% discount" looks like this:

```
print ("You receive a 95 \% discount");
```

VARIABLES

The next thing that you need to learn about are things called *variables*. Variables are parts of PERL programming that are used to store bits of information such as the name of a patron, an address, or a book request. There are two types of variables: scalar and array.

SCALAR VARIABLES

Scalar variables can hold one single piece of information— a number, word, or phrase— and can be of any length. A scalar variable looks like this:

$name

Hint: While the name of the variable cannot include any spaces, there is no problem using spaces in a value.

In this example the $ symbol tells the computer that it will be working with a scalar variable and the text is the name of a particular variable. The word "name" can be replaced with almost any other word or letter. Avoid punctuation marks and spaces in variable names.

To assign data to a scalar variable, place the scalar variable on the left, then an equal sign and finally the value you want to assign to the variable.

$x = "hello world";
$a = 16;
$cnt = 0;

The process of assigning a value to a variable is known as "initializing a variable." If you want to store a group of words in a scalar variable you will need to enclose the text in quotes.

Here are a few more examples of assigning data to a scalar variable:

$movie = "I like movies";
$oops = "I have 120 overdue books";

What Do Scalar Variables Do?

Since you have a basic idea what scalar variables are and how they are structured, you're ready to learn what they do inside CGI scripts. In Chapters 6 and 7 you learned about HTML forms and the unique name for each form element. When you submit a form it activates a corresponding PERL script. The data from the form sent to the PERL program will create a scalar variable that looks like this: *$in{'name'},* where the name is the name that you assigned to the form element. The value a visitor enters into, or selects from, a form element is the value that is assigned to the corresponding scalar variable. Perhaps the following example will make this clearer:

I create an HTML form with a single-line text box that is named "TITLE." A visitor types "A Hot Time in the Old Town Tonight" in this text box and submits the form to my Web server. My Web server will receive this information and my PERL script will create a scalar variable named *$in{'TITLE'}* containing the value "A Hot Time in the Old Town Tonight."

$in{'TITLE'} = "A Hot Time in the Old Town Tonight"

Data submitted by a visitor will always be in the form of scalar variables. There is, however, another important type of variable in PERL, an array variable.

ARRAY VARIABLES

Scalar variables can only hold one piece of information. There will be many cases, though, when you will need to retrieve and store multiple pieces of information, such as a list of titles. In PERL, you can do this by creating an array variable. Array variables can store multiple pieces of information.

An array variable will look like this:

@name

The word "name" can be replaced with almost any single word or letter you want (similar to a scalar variable) but array variable may not start with an _ , a number, or contain a period. The process of assigning values to array variables is slightly different than assigning them to scalar variables. You assign a series of values separated by commas to the right of the equal sign. All values are surrounded by a set of parentheses.

@apples = (1, 2, 3, 5, 10, "blue");
@reserve_books = ("A Time to Kill," "Sum of All Fears," County Time");

The values you assign to variables can be alpha and/or numeric.

Accessing the Values in an Array Variable

An array variable is just like a collection of scalar variables. This diagram shows you how the different values entered for a single array variable are stored in your PERL program.

1st entry	2nd entry	3rd entry
Number 0	Number 1	Number 2
A Time to Kill	Sum of All Fears	County Time

Each of the different values is stored in its own separate space. These separate storage spaces are called *array elements*. An array element stores information almost exactly like a scalar variable—it can hold any one piece of information. The first element in an array is always element Number 0, the second is element Number 1, etc.

There will be times when you may want to access an individual value stored in an array variable. To do this simply:

1. Change the @ symbol to a $.
2. Specify the array variable name.
3. Add the position number of the element to be accessed in square brackets.

Following are samples from the previous chart:

$reserve_books[0] = "A Time to Kill"
$reserve_books[1] = "Sum of All Fears"
$reserve_books[2] = "County Time"

ASSIGNING VALUES FROM ONE VARIABLE TO ANOTHER VARIABLE

As your PERL programs become more advanced you will also need to assign values from one variable to another.

The PERL code for assigning the value of one scalar variable to another scalar variable is:

$var1 = $var2;

This line of code, says *$var1* is equal to *$var2* (the value in *$var2* is assigned to *$var1*) regardless of what value *$var2* originally holds.

To illustrate this, imagine that *$var1* is currently equal to Dave and *$var2* = Paul, after the line *$var1 = $var2* both *$var1* and *$var2* will be equal to Paul.

The PERL code for assigning a value from an array variable to a scalar variable works in much the same way. The scalar variable is placed on the left side of the equal sign and the array variable on the right. Be sure to specify the single element of the array variable that you want to assign to the scalar variable. In this case we are assigning the value stored in element 1 of @*reserve_books to $my_reserve.*

$my_reserve = $reserve_books[1];

The value in *$my_reserve* is equal to the value that was being stored in *reserve_books[1]*.

The PERL code for assigning the values from multiple scalar variables to one array variable is only slightly different than assigning values to an array variable.

To assign values to an array variable our code looks like this:

@my_list (1,2,"apple", "orange");

To assign scalar variables to an array, replace items like 1, 2, apple, etc., with the names of the scalar variables.

@my_list ($var1, $var2, $tomato);

WHAT YOU'VE LEARNED SO FAR

At this point you know a little more about the structure of CGI scripts. You have worked with the program header, print function, and learned about the different types of variables that you are going to need when you start writing a CGI script to process HTML forms. Remember that the first element of all scripts must be the header, without which your script will not work. You then learned about scalar and array variables and how values are assigned to each of them. What you have learned so far is that while the library user sees what you created with HTML, the PERL script is what makes the program actually work. For example, you could create a word processing template and simply by changing the values of the variables, you could generate new forms for your library with summer hours or a new loan period. You also have the tools, that is, the PERL variables, that process information that patrons key into online forms such as a request to borrow a book for three weeks rather than two. Much of the information presented here will become clearer as you actually start creating your first PERL script.

TEST YOUR KNOWLEDGE

- The first element of an array variable is Number 0. True/False

- CGI scripts can be run from any directory. True/False

- A scalar variable *($var)* can hold multiple pieces of information (elements). True/False

- What is the value of the requested item?

  $used_car = "blue"
  @cars = ("1" ,"red", "$used_car");
  $cars[2] = ?????

- You cannot assign the value from one scalar variable to another. True/False

Answers

- **True.** Array variable elements begin with the number 0.
- **False.** CGI Scripts need to be placed in the CGI-BIN directory in order to be run.
- **False.** A scalar variable can only hold one piece of information.
- **Blue.** The value blue is assigned to the scalar variable *$used_car.* The value stored *$used_car* is then assigned the third element of the @*cars* variable.
- **False.** You can assign values from one scalar variable to another.

ESSENTIAL PERL FUNCTIONS

If all that you could do with PERL was assign values to variables, PERL would not be a very useful programming language, as your programs would not be able to complete complex tasks. Assigning values actually just scratches the surface of what PERL can do. PERL contains a number of built-in functions including printing, searching, reading, and writing to files. This next section will cover the functions most essential for creating PERL scripts that process Web forms.

THE *PRINT* FUNCTION REVISITED

Earlier in this chapter you learned the basics of the print function. To fully utilize this function you'll need to mix text and scalar variables into single print statements. To do this, place the scalar variable at the point in the print statement that you want to insert the value contained by the scalar variable.

The following code creates a print statement containing both text and scalar variables:

```
$my_reserve = "The End of Time";
print ("Thank you for placing a reserve on $my_reserve.");
print ("You will be notified when your copy is available.");
```

These lines of code will display "Thank you for placing a reserve on The End of Time. You will be notified when your copy is available." on the screen.

THE *GREP* FUNCTION

The grep function is designed to simplify text searching. Using the grep function it is easy to search an array or file for any particular text string. You can use the grep function to create an online search tool. Grep searches an array variable holding data. If it finds a match, the line containing the matched string will be added to a "found list," if the line does not match, the grep function will move to the next line looking for the requested text string. This process continues until grep reaches the end of the array variable.

In the example below, the line begins with *@found* that is the found list (the array variable where matching lines will be stored). Next is the grep command and the required commands. These commands are */search pattern/* (the character string that you want grep to match) and array to be searched (the array variable you want grep to search).

Format for the grep command:

```
@found = grep (/search pattern/, @list_to_be_searched);
```

This next example should help to illustrate this further. In the following example the grep function is searching a list of users for the name "Cara Morelli." Any time that it finds a mention of that name, the list entry containing the name will be added to an array named *@matched*. After grep reaches the end of the list of users, *@matched* is printed to the screen.

```
@matched= grep (/Cara Morelli/, @users);
print ("@matched");
```

What you have is a basic keyword search program that allows visitors to search for a single word or text string anywhere in a list of items.

THE *LENGTH* FUNCTION

The length function tells you the number of characters present in a scalar variable or in a single element of an array variable. You can use this function to see if visitors have entered data in all required fields of a form. The coding for the length function is simple:

```
length ($variable);
```

Take a look at this example:

```
$my_var = "lobster";
$number_of_characters = length ($my_var);
```

The scalar variable $number\_of\_characters$ will be assigned seven (7), the number of characters in the value assigned to the scalar variable my_var.

WHAT YOU'VE LEARNED SO FAR

These are the three essential PERL functions that you need to know to write CGI scripts: *print, grep,* and *length.* These functions will enable you to search, provide feedback to visitors, and begin to evaluate the information submitted through your forms.

While the *grep* command organizes the commands, the print command allows you to respond to the user. Remember that the print command is not confined to printing on paper, it also will print an e-mail message to print to the screen. Thus you could use it to e-mail a patron that a reserve book is in, print that same notice to send through the mail, or simply to print a "thank you" to the screen if a patron uses one of your online suggestion forms.

TEST YOUR KNOWLEDGE

- One print statement can be used to print both text and scalar variables. True/False

- Find the error in this line:

    @hits= grep ("Bruce Haynes" , @card_holders);

- The length function cannot be used to verify that visitors have completed required fields in a form. True/False

---

- **False.** The length function is an excellent way to verify that visitors have completed required fields.
- Line should be *@hits=grep (/Bruce Haynes/ , @card_holders);*
- **True.** A single print statement can print text and the content of scalar variables.

Answers

Hint: Conditional statements can be used for a variety of library functions, to send messages to the screen, such as book checked out, or to generate notices, such as an overdue notice that is printed when the number of days a book is checked out exceeds a preestablished number.

CONDITIONAL STATEMENTS (*IF, ELSIF, ELSE*)

For the most part, computer programs run from top to bottom. The computer executes one line of code and then moves on to the next, continuing on to the end of the program. There will be times when you will need to change the way a program runs. One way to control the way a program runs is to use conditional statements. A conditional statement instructs the computer to do something special if a preset condition exists. In this next section you'll learn about some of the most useful conditional statements: *if*, *elsif*, and *else*. Once you have programmed your system to act on specified conditions, you can provide more information to the library user. For example, if the message "This title is not checked out" is going to make sense when it appears on the screen, the computer needs to verify whether the condition "not checked out" has been met.

But, before learning about conditional statements, you must first learn to understand and use comparison operators. A *comparison operator* compares two things to each other. The chart below lists the common comparison operators.

COMPARISON OPERATORS

==	Equal to
<=	Less than or equal to
>=	Greater than or equal to
<	Less than
>	Greater than
!=	Not equal to

These operators are used to ask questions like:

is $x GREATER THAN $y
is $my_var EQUAL TO 30
is $input NOT EQUAL TO $output

IF . . . ELSE STATEMENTS

If and *else* statements are used to control the flow of the program. They determine how the program will react, based on the status of a piece of information when the program is run. An *if* statement tells the PERL script to do something if the statement is true.

The standard coding for an *if* statement is:

if (condition to be evaluated)
{ instructions to execute ;}

Below is a sample *if* statement that says that if *$x* is equal to 10 then display *$x = 10*. (If *$x* were equal to 13 the condition would be false and the number would not be displayed on the screen.)

if ($x == 10)
{print ("\$x = 10");}

Likewise if a book status has a numerical value, for example a 1 in the field means a book is checked out, *if . . . else* statements can cause a message ("Book checked out") to print on the screen if that field equals 1. You will use *if* statements in many places when writing PERL code. Since an *if* statement is only executed when something is true, there needs to be a way to handle statements that are not true. When you need to test for a failed *if* statement, use the *else* statement. An *else* statement must be used in conjunction with an *if* statement. It will execute only when an *if* statement is not true.

The standard coding for an *else* statement is:

else {instructions to execute if the if statement is false ;}

Take a look at an expanded version of the previous *if* statement. In this case, if the value of *$x* is not equal to 10, then the *else* statement will execute instead.

if ($x == 10)
{ print ("\$x = 10");}
else {print ("\$x is not equal to 10");}

THE "IF . . . ELSE" MANTRA

If *this is true then do something* . . . else *do something else.*

TEST YOUR KNOWLEDGE

What do these statements mean?

- *if ($a ==3)*
  {print ("OK");

- *if (length ($name < 2)*
  {print ("Please complete the name field to continue");}

- *if ($a != 3)*
  {print ("The variable is not equal to three");}

Answers

- If $a is equal to 3 the computer will print OK.
- This next example incorporates part of last chapter with the use of the *length* function in the *if* statement. It will be true if the length of the data stored in *$name* is less than two.
- This statement will evaluate as true if *$a* is not equal to 3.

ELSIF STATEMENTS

By now you should be able to understand how to use *if . . . else* statements to test if something is true or not, so that your PERL program can execute one of two options based on the evaluation. *If . . . else* statements can be further expanded with the addition of *elsif.* Using the *elsif* statement you can test for multiple conditions allowing your program to take various actions, depending on how the statement is evaluated. To add this enhanced capability to your program you will use an *elsif* (else if) statement.

The standard coding for an *elsif* statement is:

```
elsif (condition to be tested)
{code to execute if true;}
```

To function properly, this statement must come in the middle of an *if . . . else* statement. This next example will illustrate.

```
if ($x == 3)
{print ("The answer is 3");}
elsif ($x < 3)
{print ("The answer is less than 3");}
else
{print ("The answer is greater than 3");}
```

This sample produces a program with three possible paths of execution. When the program examines the first statement *if ($x ==3),* if this statement is true, the computer will display "The answer is 3" on the screen and the program will jump to the next line of code after the end of the *else* statement and continue to run.

If the statement if *($x==3)* is not true, the program will move on to the next statement *elsif($x < 3)*. This will be evaluated. If it is true, the computer will display "The answer is less than 3" on the screen. If it is not true, the *else* statement will be executed and the computer will display "The answer is greater than 3" on the screen.

Conditional statements are very useful tools that you will use frequently as you write PERL programs. But they are not the only way to control how programs run.

CREATING LOOPS

Loops are parts of programs that can repeat themselves multiple times. As loops repeat themselves they will repeatedly execute a set of instructions. Loops must also have an exit condition, something that tells the computer when to stop executing the loop. Even though loops are not overly complex, they do require careful attention.

WHILE LOOPS

A *while* loop is a section of code that will be repeated as long as the exit condition has not been reached.

The coding for the *while* loop is:

```
while (exit condition)
{
Code to do something, may be as long as you like.
}
```

The coding below creates a *while* loop that will print the different values that are going to be assigned to *$x*. The additional line of code you see *$x++;* tells the computer to take the value that is in *$x* and add one to it. This is the same as the notation *$x=$x+1* but it is easier to write. The line *$x++;* acts like a counter. Each time the loop runs, the value in *$x* is increased by 1. When *$x* is no longer less than 10 the loop stops and the program moves on to the line of code after the *while* loop.

```
while ($x , 10)
{
     print ("x = $x");
$x++;
     }
```

This loop will run 10 times displaying:

```
x=
x=1
x=2
x=3
x=4
x=5
x=6
```

Hint: Beginning programmers often create programs with loops that don't include an exit condition. These loops run indefinitely, consuming large amounts of server memory and processing time, and possibly even crashing the server.

Hint: Loops will not only provide protection from hackers by shutting the system down if certain commands are received, but also decrease your programming burden by allowing you to return to a command or series of commands rather than enter them again.

Hint: Always remember to assign a value to your variables before using them in a loop. Never assign a value inside a loop.

x=7
x=8
x=9

These next two examples show the right and wrong way to do this.

RIGHT

```
$x = 0;
while ($x < 10)
    { print ("Hello World");
    $x++;
    }
```

WRONG

```
while ($x < 10)
{ $x = 0;
    print (" Hello World");
    $x++; }
```

In the incorrectly coded example, each time the *while* loop executes, *$x* is reset to 0; therefore, the exit condition is never reached and the loop will never stop running. Note that in the correct way the line *$x = 0;* is placed before the *while* loop.

FOR LOOPS

Another type of loop is the *for* loop. *For* loops allow you to put all parts controlling the loop (variable initialization, conditional statement, and loop counter) into one line of code.

The standard coding used in a *for* loop is:

```
for (initialize variable; exit condition; loop counter)
{
code . . . . . . . . . .
}
```

The first line may look somewhat confusing, but it really isn't.
- The first part of the line *$x=1* gives the variable *$x* a value of one.
- The second part of the line *$x < 10* tells the computer what to check before executing this loop; in this case the program checks to see if *$x* is still less than 10.
- The final part of this line is *$x++*. This tells the computer that each time the loop executes, the value in *$x* should be increased by one.

You will notice that the line with the print statement below contains a new symbol \n, which is the new line character. This character tells the program, when it is printing, to move to the next line before printing more text (sort of like the <BR> tag in HTML).

```
for ($x = 1; $x < 10; $x++)
{
print ("Hello World \n");
}
```

TEST YOUR KNOWLEDGE

- Look at this sample coding that includes a *for* loop. What will be displayed on the screen after the loop finishes running?

```
#! usr/local/bin/perl
push(@INC,"/data1/ip/iubks/cgi-bin/");
require ("cgi-lib.pl");
&ReadParse;
print &PrintHeader;
$x = "hello world";
$y = 4;

for ($a = 1; $a <= $y; $a++)
{print ("$x\n");}
```

- See if you can locate the error in this next section of code.

```
$a= 0;
for ($b = 1; $b > $a; $b++)
{print ("OOPS! \n");}
```

Answers

- *hello world* will display on the screen four times.
- The value of $a is set to 0. This means that $b will always be greater and that the loop will never stop executing.

WHAT YOU'VE LEARNED SO FAR

This section introduced some of the most important concepts you will encounter when writing PERL code: comparison operators (== , < , >, etc.), conditional statements (*if, elsif, else*), and loops (*while* and *for*). You will use these many times when writing programs to process HTML forms.

WORKING WITH FILES

OPENING FILES

In order to read data from files stored on your Web server or to record information submitted by visitors, you will need to create a PERL program that is able to read and write to files. Before you start working with files, be sure you have the necessary file "permissions" to read and write files to your Web server. (If not, ask your "techie" to set this up for you.)

Then, you'll need to learn how to open the files you want to work with. The command for opening a file is:

open (reference name, "filename");

- The line begins with the *open* command.
- The reference name is the name that you will use to refer to the file in your CGI script. Most programmers elect to use the word FILE in all capital letters as the reference name.
- Filename is the name of the file that you want to open.

In the example below, FILE is the reference name and the name of the file to be opened is *"test_file.txt."*

open (FILE, "test_file.txt");

SELECTING AN ACCESS MODE

When you open a file you must select an access mode. Access modes tell your computer what you intend to do with a file. There are three file access modes in PERL: read, write, and append.

Read *Access Mode*

This mode allows you to read the contents of a file, but not to change the contents of the file. The PERL code to open a file in read mode is:

open (FILE, "data.txt")

This will probably be the most common mode of file access used in your PERL scripts.

Write *File Access Mode*

This mode allows you to replace the contents of a file.

The PERL coding to open a file (note the single >) in write mode is:

open (FILE, ">filename");

Hint: You must be very careful when using the "write" mode because all the contents of your original file will be erased when you use this mode. Be sure that you have a backup of the file before starting to work in the "write" mode.

Append *File Access Mode*

This access mode opens your file in a manner that allows you to add data to the end of the file. Unlike the "write" mode, the "append" mode does not destroy the contents of the file, it only adds information to the end of the file.

The PERL coding to open a file (note the double **>>**) in append mode:

open (FILE, ">>filename");

Before you open a file in any of these modes it is wise to make a backup of it. There are no "safety nets" when dealing with PERL scripts. It is possible to destroy the contents of a file and not even know what happened.

CLOSING FILES

You now know how to open file; you also need to be able to close them to prevent them from becoming corrupted.

The command to close a file is:

close (reference_name);

This next example below shows a file being opened in read mode and then closed:

open (FILE, "my_file.html");
close (FILE);

The next procedure is to read a file and store the contents of the file in an array variable.

> **Hint:** The best way to protect your data is to develop a routine: open a file, work with the file, and then close it as quickly as possible.

READING FILES

Once a file has been opened in read mode you will need to place information in the file. There are two methods for reading files: one line at a time, or all at once.

To read one line from a file you'll use a scalar variable to hold the data. In the following example the scalar variable *$temp* is assigned the data read from the first line of FILE.

open (FILE, "temp.txt");
$temp = <FILE>;
close (FILE);

To read the contents of the entire file into the program you'll use an array variable. This program reads the contents of the file "my_file.txt" and stores it in the *array @whole_file*. Each line of the file is treated as an element of the variable *@whole_file*.

open (FILE, "my_file.txt");
@whole_file = <FILE>;
close (FILE);

TROUBLESHOOTING: INCLUDING THE DIE FUNCTION

If your program is to open a file named "my_file.txt" what would happen if that file had been deleted or didn't exist? The program would not access files correctly, possibly resulting in missing or corrupted data. You can use an *if . . . else* statement to check that a file has been opened correctly. If it has not, the else condition will stop the program and tell the user that there was an error.

This example will illustrate the concept.

```
#! usr/local/bin/perl
push(@INC,/"data1/ip/iubks/cgi-bin/");
require ("cgi-lib.pl");
&ReadParse;
print &PrintHeader;
if (open (FILE, "my_file.txt"))
        {
                @whole_file = <FILE>;
close (FILE);
                print @whole_file;
                }
else

                {
                print ("A serious error has occurred, contact the administrator");
                die ( );
                }
```

The previous example introduces a new PERL function, *die*. When trying to open a file, if the file does not open, you need the program to immediately stop to avoid creating more serious errors. You can use the *die* function to stop the execution of your program at any point. The sample code uses a standard *if . . . else* test to see if the file opens successfully. If so, everything works fine; otherwise the else statement will be executed and the program will stop running. This else statement includes the *die* function and a print statement displays an error message before the program stops.

WRITING TO FILES

Writing information to a file allows you to take the information submitted by visitors or created by your PERL program and add it to a file stored on your Web server. To start writing to a file you will need to open the file in "write" or "append" mode.

Using Write *Mode*

Let's first look at opening a file in write mode and then writing data to that file. Remember that opening a file in write mode will destroy the contents of a file, if the file already exists; if not, PERL will create a new file. To write new data to this file you will use the print function with a slight modification.

Instead of typing:

print ("hello world");

which would display "hello world" on the screen, you will type:

print FILE("hello world");

To print information to a file use the reference name FILE right after the word PRINT in the print command. What you have printed will not be displayed on the screen, instead it will be stored in a file. You can still use variables in print commands, so coding like *print FILE ("$my_var");* also will work.

To create a new file and add text "hello world" to that file:

open (FILE, ">new_file.txt");
print FILE ("hello world \n");

The sample script below uses the write access mode to overwrite the file called *"my_file.txt"*. It then writes two lines of text to this file before the close command is issued. If the file *"my_file.txt"* cannot be created or overwritten the program will execute the *die* command.

```
#! usr/local/bin/perl
push(@INC,"/data1/ip/iubks/cgi-bin/");
require ("cgi-lib.pl");
&ReadParse;
print &PrintHeader;
$holder = "Your library books are overdue!!!!!";
if (open (FILE, ">my_file.txt"))
{ print FILE ("Hello there \n");
          print FILE ("$holder");
    close (FILE);
}
else {print ("A serious error has occurred");
          die( );}
```

USING *APPEND* MODE

Often you will want to add data to the end of a file. To do this, use the "append" file mode. The only change in the appearance of the program will be in the line used to open the file.

Write *mode*

open (FILE, ">my_file.txt");

Append *mode*

```
open (FILE, ">>my_file.txt");
```

The addition of one "greater than" sign is the only difference between write and append access modes. The example below opens the file *"notes.txt"* in append mode and adds the text *"Problem Patron"* to the last line of this file.

```
#! usr/local/bin/perl
push(@INC,"/data1/ip/iubks/cgi-bin/");
require ("cgi-lib.pl");
&ReadParse;
print &PrintHeader;
if (open (FILE, ">>notes.txt")
    {
            print FILE ("Problem Patron");
close (FILE);
}
else

            {
            print ("A serious error has occurred");
            die( );
            }
```

PATTERN MATCHING

One of PERL's most useful features is its ability to do complex pattern matching. This allows you to look for certain sequences of characters in a string of text. Pattern matching can be rather confusing at first, but give it a chance. If you've made it this far you'll catch on quickly.

The basic format for pattern matching is:

```
$var_to_be_searched =~ /pattern to look for/;
```

The =~ symbol signifies that you are looking for a pattern match.
The example below will search the variable *$my_string* for the letters "abc."

```
$my_string =~ /abc/;
```

You'll often want to combine pattern matching with *if . . . else* tests. The code below assumes that form input allows visitors to indicate their preferred method of contact. The pattern match then elicits the correct response when the visitor indicates they prefer a particular contact method.

```
if ($method_of_contact =~ /Email/;)
{print ("Glad to see you've got Email");}
else {print ("Why Don't You Get an Email address?! ");}
```

There may also be occasions when you will need to know if a pattern does not match. Just replace =~ with !~ the PERL symbol for "does not match."

Here are some symbols that will help you do pattern matching.

[ ] Allows you to specify a range of characters to be matched. /B[ae]ll/ This will match either the word "ball" or "bell."

[^] All characters EXCEPT those following the caret are to be matched. /[^ABC]/ This matches any letter other than "A", "B", or "C."

\d Matches any digit.

\D Anything *not* a digit (letters and symbols).

\w Any word character, includes numbers and letters but not punctuation or white space

\W Any non-word character

\s Matches white space.

\S Matches anything that is not white space.

These symbol combinations can save you some time and reduce the complexity of your programs. Both of the two pattern matching examples below produce identical results, but note the difference in complexity.

$area =~ /[1234567890]/;
or
$area =~ /\d/;

SUBSTITUTION

A variation of pattern matching is called *substitution*, the locating and replacing of text. The coding for substitution is very similar to pattern matching:

Pattern matching

$my_book =~/abc/;

Substitution

$my_book =~s/abc/xyz/;

The *s* before the first / tells PERL that this will be a substitution operation. Following the first slash is the pattern that you are looking for. Following the second slash is the text that will replace the pattern that was found. This may sound confusing but look at the following example, it should help to clarify the concept.

$my_book = "Body Firm";
$my_book =~ s/Body/My/;

$my_book equals *"My Firm"*.

WHAT YOU'VE LEARNED SO FAR

- There are three different access modes (*read, write,* and *append*).
- The *read* mode allows you to read the contents of a file, but you can't change the contents of the file.
- The *write* mode will overwrite the contents of the original file.
- The *append* access mode will allow you to add data to the end of the file.
- The *die* function helps you handle errors by stopping the program.
- Pattern matching and substitution allow you to locate and/or replace text.

These are the commands you will use to change the wording on an overdue notice or to change the hours on a library flier.

HANDLING DATA FROM HTML FORMS

Now that you know a little about PERL, it's time for you to learn how HTML forms relate to PERL scripts. To develop CGI programs, you'll need to be able to accept input from the form a visitor sends you and then use that data in your script. Remember when you created a form, you gave names to each of the form's elements? It's now time to set up your PERL scripts to recognize these names and correctly use the information supplied by your form.

Most HTML form element names are usually pretty descriptive as to the data they contain. For example, the name of a field that contains a person's name will probably be "name." When a form sends data to a PERL program each element is converted into a scalar variable.

Each form element name will change from a simple word to the form in the example ·below:

Element in HTML Form	Element converted to PERL scalar variable
name	*$in{'name'}*
date	*$in{'date'}*

Each form element will be assigned a unique name with *$in{' '}* being added to their original names to create a PERL scalar variable.

COMPARING AN HTML FORM AND ITS CORRESPONDING PERL SCRIPT

These next two sections of code will illustrate the relationship between an HTML form and a PERL program. You will see how the variables in the form become part of the PERL program and are used. All of the variable names in both pieces of code will be in boldface type.

HTML Form to Demonstrate Variable Relationships

```
<HTML>
<HEAD>
<TITLE>Sample Form to show relationship of Web forms and PERL CGI-
BIN programs </TITLE>
</HEAD>
<BODY BGCOLOR="CAAAAF">
<FONT SIZE=6> Sample ILL Form</FONT>
<HR SIZE=6 NOSHADE>
<FORM METHOD=POST ACTION=HTTP://198.30.145.82/CGI-BIN/
TESTME.PL>
<TABLE CELLPADDING=6>
<TR><TD COLSPAN=4><CENTER><FONT SIZE=5>Item Information
<TR><TD><FONT SIZE=4>Name of Item:
<TD> <INPUT TYPE ="TEXT" NAME="Item">
<TD><FONT SIZE=4>Author:
<TD><INPUT TYPE="TEXT" NAME="Author">
<TR><TD><FONT SIZE=4>Date of Publication:
<TD><INPUT TYPE="TEXT" NAME="Date_of_pub">
<TD><FONT SIZE=4>Pages Needed:
<TD><INPUT TYPE="TEXT" NAME="Pages">
<TR><TD COLSPAN=4><CENTER><FONT SIZE=5>Patron Information
<TR><TD><FONT SIZE=4>Patron Name:
<TD><INPUT TYPE="TEXT" NAME="User_name">
<TD><FONT SIZE=4>Library Card Number:
<TD><INPUT TYPE="TEXT" NAME="Card_number">
<TR><TD><FONT SIZE=4>Phone Number:
<TD><INPUT TYPE="TEXT" NAME="Phone">
<TD><FONT SIZE=4>E-mail address:
<TD><INPUT TYPE="TEXT" NAME="Email">
<TR><TD><FONT SIZE=4>Date item is needed by:
<TD><INPUT TYPE="TEXT" NAME="Need_date">
</TABLE></CENTER>
<INPUT TYPE="SUBMIT" VALUE="SUBMIT INFORMATION">
<INPUT TYPE="RESET" VALUE="CLEAR INFORMATION">
</FORM>
```

This example shows an abbreviated form of coding in which the table tags are not expressed as tag pairs. This type of coding works, so use it to save yourself lots of additional typing.

PERL Script to Demonstrate Variable Relationships

A working version
of this script can be
found on the CD-
ROM in the PERL
folder under **8.pl.**

```perl
#! usr/local/bin/perl
push(@INC,"/data1/ip/iubks/cgi-bin/");
require "cgi-lib.pl";
&ReadParse;
print &PrintHeader;

#write user supplied data to file
if (open (FILE,">>requests.txt"))
    {print FILE "Item name: $in{'Item'} \n");
        print FILE "Author: $in{'Author'} \n");
    print FILE "Date of Publication: $in{'Date_of_pub'} \n");
    print FILE "Pages: $in{'Pages'} \n");
    print FILE "Requester name: $in{'User_name'} \n");
    print FILE "Requester card number: $in{'Card_number'} \n");
    print FILE "Phone: $in{'Phone'} \n");
    print FILE "E-mail: $in{'Email'} \n");
    print FILE "Needed by: $in{'Need_date'} \n");
    close (FILE);
    }
else {
        print "Program Error, request not be processed. Please contact");
        print "technical support");
        die ( );}

# program only reaches this point if the file opened successfully
print "<font size = 4>Thank you for submitting your request.");
print "It will be reviewed by the library staff <br>");
print "You will be contacted when the item has arrived.");
```

WHAT YOU'VE LEARNED SO FAR

At this point you should feel comfortable with many of the basics of PERL programming.

You should understand how to:

- Initialize and use both scalar and array variables.
- Print information to a visitor's computer screen.
- Search for information using *grep*.
- Use *if . . . else* statements to control program flow.
- Write loops using *while* and *for*.
- *Read* and *write* information from files.
- Terminate a program.
- Collect information submitted by HTML forms.

TEST YOUR KNOWLEDGE

- Write a PERL script that opens a file and reads from it. If it fails, it should die and return an error message to you.

- Write a PERL script using a *for* loop that does the following:

  Asks you for a number and then prints that number and the next four numbers following it. (You enter 9, and the program will print 9, 10, 11, 12, and 13.)

9

PERL and Web Forms

By now you should have a good foundation in the basics of PERL and are now ready to create some useful CGI scripts that will greatly enhance your Web site.

In this section you will learn how to write programs that are able to:

- Store and retrieve information submitted by visitors to your Web site
- Allow patrons to submit information and requests using a Web form and have that information sent as an e-mail message to a library staff member.
- Address the security issues associated with developing and implementing PERL scripts on your Web server.
- Look up information in a database using a PERL-based CGI script.

STORING AND RETRIEVING DATA FROM FORMS

In Chapter 8 you learned the basic tools for getting visitor input from forms and reading and writing files. The following program will combine both operations, creating a form that asks for and records visitor input. User feedback forms are a common form type that will help to illustrate how the HTML form and its corresponding PERL script work together to provide both you and visitors with information. The feedback HTML form below enables patrons to rate the performance of staff. Form ratings are then sent to a matching PERL script, which stores the information in a file on your Web server, allowing library staff members to access and analyze the data at a later time. To create the feedback form:

Step 1: Develop the HTML form.

Step 2: Write a PERL script to deal with the information gathered by the form.

Step 3: Run the program and store the retrieved data in a file on your Web server.

CREATING A USER FEEDBACK FORM

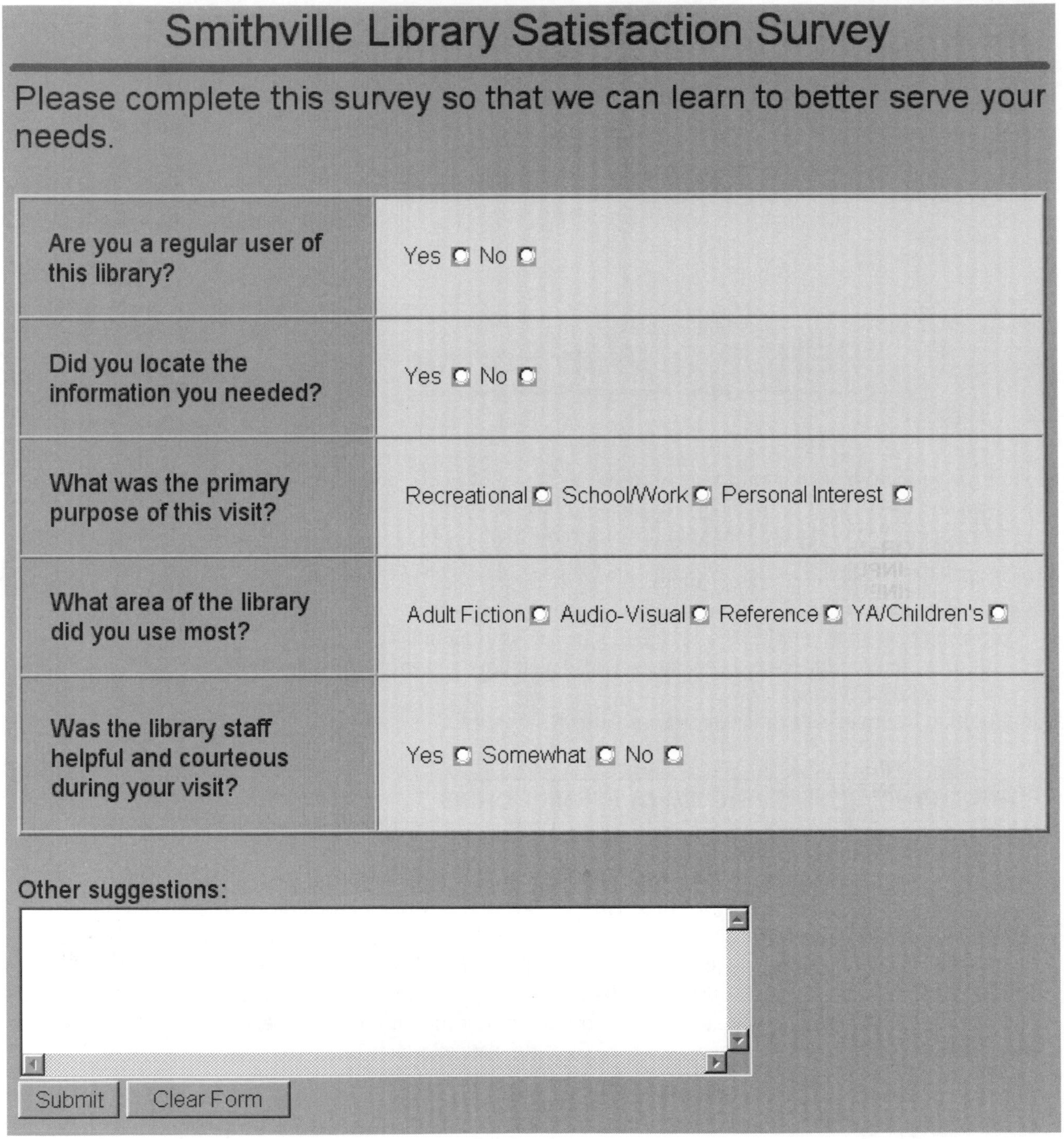

Smithville Library Satisfaction Survey

Please complete this survey so that we can learn to better serve your needs.

Are you a regular user of this library?	Yes ○ No ○
Did you locate the information you needed?	Yes ○ No ○
What was the primary purpose of this visit?	Recreational ○ School/Work ○ Personal Interest ○
What area of the library did you use most?	Adult Fiction ○ Audio-Visual ○ Reference ○ YA/Children's ○
Was the library staff helpful and courteous during your visit?	Yes ○ Somewhat ○ No ○

Other suggestions:

[Submit] [Clear Form]

Figure 9–1: User Feedback Form

FEEDBACK FORM IN HTML

```html
<HTML>
<HEAD>
<TITLE>Smithville Library Satisfaction Survey</TITLE>
</HEAD>
<BODY BGCOLOR="AACFCF">
<CENTER><FONT SIZE=6>Smithville Library Satisfaction Survey</FONT></CENTER>
<HR SIZE=6 NOSHADE>
<FONT SIZE=5>Please complete this survey so that we can learn to better serve your needs.
<FORM METHOD="GET" ACTION="http://www.yourserver.com/cgi-bin/script.pl">
<TABLE BORDER=2 CELLPADDING=20 CELLSPACING=1>
<TR><TD WIDTH=20%><FONT SIZE=4>
Are you a regular user of this library?
<TD BGCOLOR="F1F1F1"><FONT SIZE=3>
Yes <INPUT TYPE="RADIO" NAME="user" VALUE="YES">
No <INPUT TYPE="RADIO" NAME="user" VALUE="NO">
<TR><TD><FONT SIZE=4>
Did you locate the information you needed?
<TD BGCOLOR="F1F1F1"><FONT SIZE=3>
Yes <INPUT TYPE="RADIO" NAME="locate" VALUE="YES">
No <INPUT TYPE="RADIO" NAME="locate" VALUE="NO">
<TR><TD><FONT SIZE=4>
What was the primary purpose of this visit?
<TD BGCOLOR="F1F1F1"><FONT SIZE=3>
Recreational<INPUT TYPE="RADIO" NAME="visit" VALUE="REC">
School/Work<INPUT TYPE="RADIO" NAME="visit" VALUE="SCHOOL">
Personal Interest <INPUT TYPE="RADIO" NAME="visit" VALUE="INTEREST">
<TR><TD><FONT SIZE=4>
What area of the library did you use most?
<TD BGCOLOR="F1F1F1"><FONT SIZE=3>
Adult Fiction<INPUT TYPE="RADIO" NAME="area" VALUE="FICTION">
Audio-Visual<INPUT TYPE="RADIO" NAME="area" VALUE="AV">
Reference<INPUT TYPE="RADIO" NAME="area" VALUE="REF">
YA/Children's<INPUT TYPE="RADIO" NAME="area" VALUE="JUV">
<TR><TD><FONT SIZE=4>
Were you satisfied with the level of service you received?
<TD BGCOLOR="F1F1F1"><FONT SIZE=3>
Yes <INPUT TYPE="RADIO" NAME="service" VALUE="YES">
Somewhat <INPUT TYPE="RADIO" NAME="service" VALUE="SOMEWHAT">
No <INPUT TYPE="RADIO" NAME="service" VALUE="NO">
<TR><TD><FONT SIZE=4>
Was the library staff helpful and courteous during your visit?
<TD BGCOLOR="F1F1F1"><FONT SIZE=3>
Yes <INPUT TYPE="RADIO" NAME="help" VALUE="YES">
Somewhat <INPUT TYPE="RADIO" NAME="help" VALUE="SOMEWHAT">
No <INPUT TYPE="RADIO" NAME="help" VALUE="NO">
</TABLE>
<P>
<FONT SIZE=4>Other suggestions:<BR>
<TEXTAREA COLS=50 ROWS=5 NAME=suggest>
</TEXTAREA><BR>
<INPUT TYPE="SUBMIT" VALUE="Submit">
<INPUT TYPE="RESET" VALUE="Clear Form">
</FORM>
</BODY>
</HTML>
```

*A working version of this form can be found on the CD-ROM in the HTML folder under **9–1.html.***

This example shows an abbreviated form of coding in which the table tags are not expressed as tag pairs. This coding method works, so use it to save yourself lots of additional typing.

A working version
of this script can
be found on the
CD-ROM in the
PERL folder under
9–1.pl.

PERL PROGRAM TO HANDLE THE FEEDBACK FORM

```perl
#! usr/local/bin/perl
push(@INC,"/http/cgi-bin/");
require ("cgi-lib.pl");
&ReadParse; print &PrintHeader;
### End of PERL header

#assign the incoming variables to more easy-to-use scalar variables.
$user = $in{'user'};
$locate = $in{'locate'};
$visit = $in{'visit'};
$area = $in{'area'};
$service = $in{'service'};
$help = $in{'help'};

#open the data file for appending, writes all of the responses to the file
open (FILE, >>response.txt);
#this next line write a dashed line to the file to help separate entries
print FILE ("_____");
print FILE (" `date` "); print FILE ("Regular User: $user \n");
print FILE ("Did you find your information: $locate \n");
print FILE ("Primary purpose of visit: $visit \n");
print FILE ("Area of library used: $area \n");
print FILE ("Satisfied with service: $service \n");
print FILE ("Courteous or Helpful: $help \n");
close FILE;

#output message to the user's screen
print ("<html><head><title>Thank you</title></head>");
print ("<body bgcolor= \"ffffff\">");
print ("Thank you for taking the time to fill out our survey.<br>");
print ("The library will use your answers to identify");
print ("areas where we can improve our service.<p>");
print ("<a href=\"main.html\">Return to Main page</a>");
print ("</body></html>");
```

This is the first fully functional HTML form/CGI script combination that you've examined.

THE *DATE* COMMAND

Almost all of the code in the previous program has been covered, except for the *date* command. When used, this command prints the current date. In the case of our survey script the date was not output to the screen but instead written to the file so that library staff will know when each form was submitted. The date command is normally combined with a print statement to produce:

```perl
print (" `date` ");
```

SECURITY CONCERNS AND SOLUTIONS

Although the first script example is useful, it brings up a number of potential security problems. What would keep visitors from sending large amounts of, or potentially dangerous, data as a response to your form and possibly crashing your server? At this point nothing. You therefore need to learn some methods of providing security for forms prior to using them in any real-life applications.

Here then, are a few tricks that will help you create programs that have a better-than-average chance of running safely.

The first thing that you can do is to check all incoming variables for length. By using the *length* function you will be able to determine how much data is being submitted. When implemented correctly, if the information submitted is too long, your program will automatically stop, thus preventing server overload. The following line of code uses an *if* test to examine the length of the data submitted. If the data is too long, the program will execute the *die* function and stop executing.

if (length ($in{'area'}) > 40){die ( );}

The *length* function can also check for a minimum amount of data in an element. This is very useful if you want to make sure particular fields in your form are filled out fully. To implement a check for the length of a variable, your code would look like this:

if (length ($in{'phone'} < 7)
{print (" Please include your complete phone number\n");
die ( );}

If the user fails to enter at least seven characters for their phone number, the program will print an error message and then stop running.

To further enhance your security, make sure that visitors always use your forms to access your CGI scripts. Many attacks on Web servers occur from hackers accessing PERL scripts directly, bypassing your HTML forms. To prevent this, examine the contents of the *$ENV{'HTTP_REFERER'}* variable to make sure that a visitor is accessing your PERL script from the HTML page you intend to have it accessed from. This variable is sent by the patron's Web browser and contains the URL of the page that submitted the form to your server. To implement this security check, make sure that the visitor's response comes from your form's URL before processing any of the information submitted. This check can be accomplished with the following *if* statement.

if ($ENV{'HTTP_REFERER'} !~/www.ohionet.org/) {die ( );}

This *if* statement looks for the pattern *"www.ohionet.org"* in the variable *$ENV{'HTTP_REFERER'}*. If this pattern is not found, the script will stop running. Since the visitor attempted to obtain unauthorized access to your system, it is advisable to record some information about the offender prior to stopping the program. The following code will give you a glimpse of who the patron is and what they tried to do.

```
if ($ENV{'HTTP_REFERER'} !~/www.ohionet.org/)
{open (FILE, ">>secure.txt");
# IP address of user's computers
print FILE ("USER IP: $ENV{'REMOTE_ADDR'}\n");
# URL from which the user submitted data
print FILE ("FROM PAGE: $ENV{'HTTP_REFERER'}\n");

# name of the visitor's computer
print FILE ("USER Comp Name: $ENV{'REMOTE_HOST'}\n");
#type of browser being used
print FILE ("USER Browser: $ENV{'HTTP_USER_AGENT'}\n");
# information was that the user entered into your form
print FILE ("QUERY: $ENV{'QUERY_STRING'}");
close (FILE);
print ("Security Violation");
die ( );
}
```

You will also need to test the variables for content, to make sure that they do not contain certain characters that could be used to hack the system. The code below prevents a user from submitting characters that can cause unintended and harmful actions to your server.

```
if ($user_var =~ /\!\@\#\%\^/ )
{print ("Invalid Character");
die ( );}
```

If a visitor sends any data to your program with these dangerous characters the program will stop running.

Leaving page 137 blank makes it possible for us to show you the keyword database search form (page 138) on a page facing the HTML coding used to create it (page 139). The PERL coding that makes it functional follows on pages 140–141.

CREATING A KEYWORD DATABASE SEARCH FORM

One very useful form that you can create using PERL, is a form that will keyword search locally maintained databases. In this next section you will learn how to create the HTML form and corresponding PERL script to keyword search a database. The first step is to create a form that provides a field for a visitor to input a keyword search term.

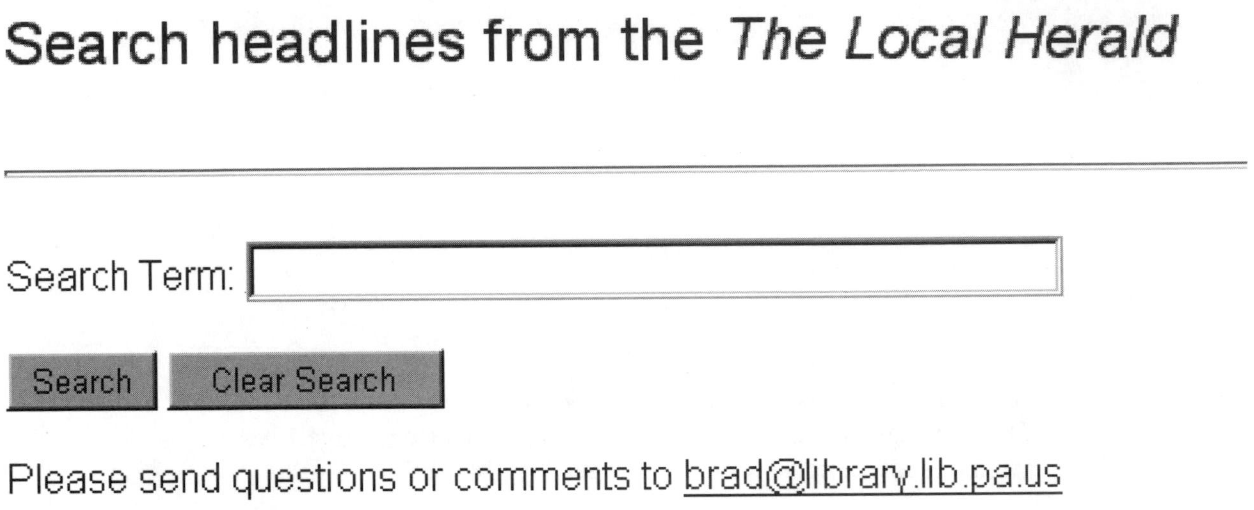

Search headlines from the *The Local Herald*

Search Term: [   ]

[Search]   [Clear Search]

Please send questions or comments to brad@library.lib.pa.us

Figure 9–2: Keyword Database Search Form

KEYWORD SEARCH FORM IN HTML

A working version of this form can be found on the CD-ROM in the HTML folder under 9–2.html.

```
<HTML>
<HEAD>
<TITLE> Keyword Search Database </TITLE>
</HEAD>
<BODY BGCOLOR="FFFFFF">
<FONT SIZE=5>Search headlines from the <I>The Local Herald</I>
</FONT><P>
<HR>
<FORM ACTION="http://www.ohionet.org/cgi-bin/keyword_test.pl"
METHOD="GET">
Search Term: <INPUT TYPE="TEXT" SIZE=40 NAME="search_term">
<P>
<INPUT TYPE="SUBMIT" VALUE="Search">
<INPUT TYPE="RESET" VALUE="Clear Search">
</FORM>
Please send questions or comments to
<A HREF="MAILTO:brad@library.lib.pa.us">brad@library.lib.pa.us</A>
</BODY>
</HTML>
```

The next step is to prepare your data. Data a visitor will be searching should be placed in the following format and stored on your server.

AUTHOR	TITLE	DATE	PAGE
#aKristin Bacon	#tLearning to Cook	#d09/23/96	#pC3
#aRoselyn Haynes	#tRunning Your Library	#d05/04/73	#pA4

A working version
of this script can
be found on the
CD-ROM in the
PERL folder under
9–2.pl.

PERL PROGRAM TO HANDLE THE DATABASE SEARCH

```
#! usr/local/bin/perl
push(@INC,"/data1/ip/iubks/cgi-bin/");
require ("cgi-lib.pl");
&ReadParse; print &PrintHeader;
#standard WWW based PERL header

#security check for dangerous characters
if ($search_term =~ /\!\@\#\%\^/ )
{print ("Invalid Character");
die ( );}

if ($ENV{'HTTP_REFERER'} !~/www.ohionet.org/)
{open (FILE, ">>secure.txt");
# IP address of user's computers
print FILE ("USER IP: $ENV{'REMOTE_ADDR'}\n");
# URL from which the user submitted data
print FILE ("FROM PAGE: $ENV{'HTTP_REFERER'}\n");

# name of the visitor's computer
print FILE ("USER Comp Name: $ENV{'REMOTE_HOST'}\n");
#type of browser being used
print FILE ("USER Browser: $ENV{'HTTP_USER_AGENT'}\n");
# information was that the user entered into your form
print FILE ("QUERY: $ENV{'QUERY_STRING'}");
close (FILE);
print ("Security Violation");
die ( );
}

#list and assign all variables, it helps to do this all at once so that you don't
#forget things later in your program

$search_term = $in{'search_term'};
$author = "<hr><br><font size=5>Author: </font>";
$title = "<br><font size=5> Title: </font>";
$date = "<br><font size=5>Date: </font>";
$page = "<br><font size=5>Page: </font>";

#this next line uses length to require the user to enter something to search
for in the #title field. if the field is blank the program will stop

if (length ($data) < 2)
    {print ("Please enter a search term for the database");
     die();
     }

### Section executes if the above if test is not true ######

# open the file in read mode
open (FILE, "news_file.txt");

#assign the data in the file to the variable@file
```

```
@file = <FILE>;

#search the variable @file for the term supplied in $search_term, results
#are assigned to @hits

@hits = grep($search_term, @file);

#check the number of hits, this will tell us the number of lines in the vari-#
#able @hits
$hits = @hits;

#kills the program if there were no hits, there is no point in continuing if
#the search had no results

if ($hits == 0)
     {print ("Sorry your search returned 0 hits, would you like to revise it
and ");
 print (" <A HREF= \"data_search.html\"> Try again </A> ");
die ();
}

# executes if there were hits
else {
     while ($cnt <= $hits)
             {@hits[$cnt] =~ s/\#a/$author/;
             @hits[$cnt] =~ s/\#t/$title/;
             @hits[$cnt] =~ s/\#d/$date/;
             @hits[$cnt] =~ s/\#p/$page/;
             $cnt ++;
             }
     }
# print the number of hits and then the search data to the screen
print ("There were $hits hits matching your search term<hr><br>");
print ("@hits");
```

Congratulations!! You've just examined your second full HTML form and PERL program pair. There are some areas of this program that can be cleaned up to allow it to function more efficiently. Were you able to see where you could use substitution operators? Without using substitution, each line of the database file would have to look like this:

```
<P>
<FONT SIZE=5>Author:</FONT>Author Name<BR>
<FONT SIZE=5>Title:</FONT>Item Title<BR>
<FONT SIZE=5>Date:</FONT>Pub Date<BR>
<FONT SIZE=5>Page:</FONT>Page number<BR>
```

By using substitution, you are able to reduce the size of your program significantly; in this case it will be 50 percent smaller!

CREATING A MATERIAL RESERVE/HOLD FORM

Many libraries have begun to integrate the Web into their daily operations by creating forms that extend their services—forms that allow patrons to submit reference questions or to put holds on materials. This next document/script pair is designed to allow patrons to place reserves on items via the Web; however, it can be easily modified to meet other needs.

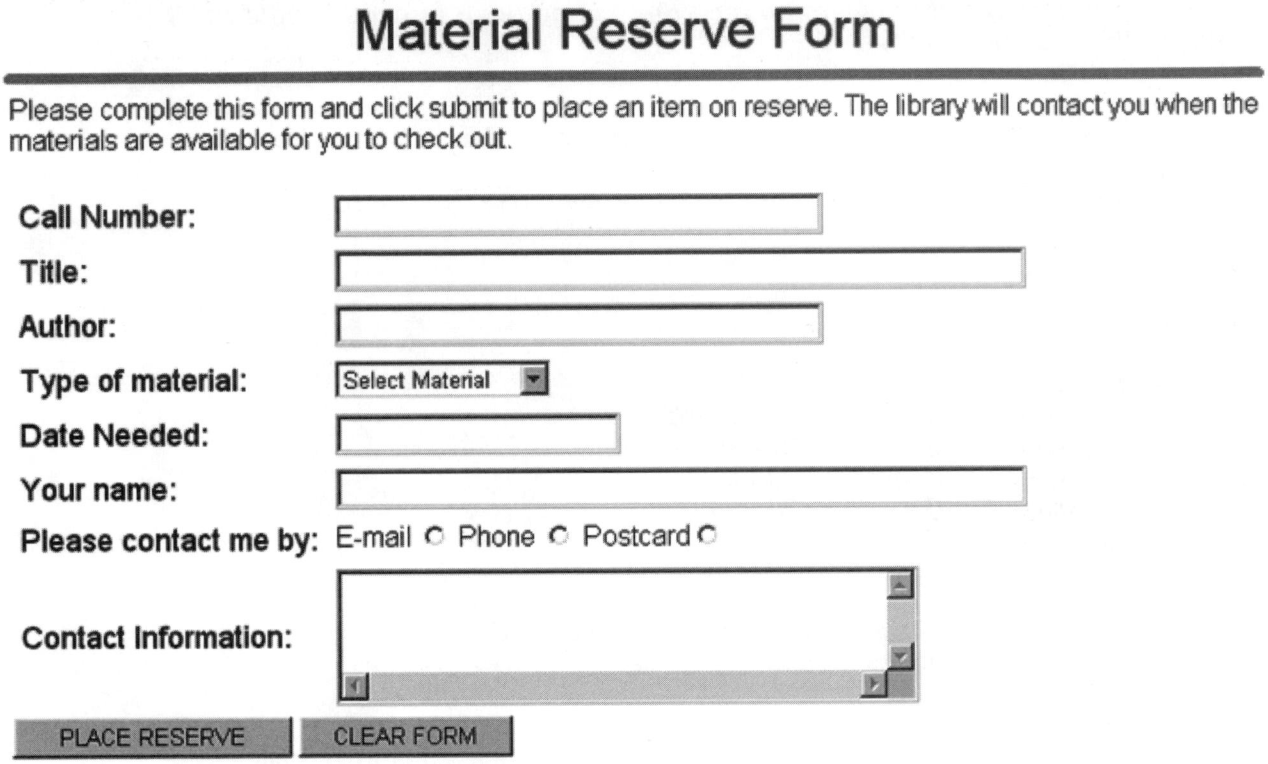

Material Reserve Form

Please complete this form and click submit to place an item on reserve. The library will contact you when the materials are available for you to check out.

Call Number:

Title:

Author:

Type of material: Select Material ▼

Date Needed:

Your name:

Please contact me by: E-mail ○ Phone ○ Postcard ○

Contact Information:

[PLACE RESERVE]   [CLEAR FORM]

Figure 9–3: Material Reserve/Hold Form

MATERIAL RESERVE/HOLD FORM IN HTML

A working version of this form can be found on the CD-ROM in the HTML folder under 9–3.html.

```
<HTML>
<HEAD>
<TITLE>Material Reserve Form</TITLE>
</HEAD>
<BODY BGCOLOR="FFFFFF">
<FONT SIZE=6><CENTER>Material Reserve Form </FONT>
<HR SIZE=6 NOSHADE>
</CENTER>
Please complete this form and click submit to place an item on reserve. The library will contact you
when the materials are available for you to check out.
<FORM ACTION="http://www.yourserver.com/cgi-bin/reserve.pl" METHOD="GET">
<TABLE>
<TR><TD><FONT SIZE=4>Call Number:
<TD><INPUT TYPE="TEXT" NAME="call_number" SIZE=35>
<TR><TD><FONT SIZE=4>Title:
<TD><INPUT TYPE="TEXT" NAME="title" SIZE=50>
<TR><TD><FONT SIZE=4>Author:
<TD><INPUT TYPE="TEXT" NAME="author" SIZE=35>
<TR><TD><FONT SIZE=4>Type of material:
<TD><SELECT NAME="material_type">
<OPTION VALUE="">Select Material
<OPTION>Hardback Book
<OPTION>Paperback Book
<OPTION>Audio Book
<OPTION>Video
<OPTION>CD (Music)
<OPTION>CD (Data)
<OPTION>Periodical
</SELECT>
<TR><TD><FONT SIZE=4>Date Needed:
<TD><INPUT TYPE="TEXT" NAME="date">
<TR><TD><FONT SIZE=4>Your name:
<TD><INPUT TYPE="TEXT" NAME="user_name" SIZE=50>
<TR><TD><FONT SIZE=4>Please contact me by:
<TD>
E-mail <INPUT TYPE="RADIO"NAME="contact"VALUE="EMAIL">
Phone <INPUT TYPE="RADIO" NAME="contact" VALUE="PHONE">
Postcard<INPUT TYPE="RADIO" NAME="contact" VALUE="POST">
<TR><TD><FONT SIZE=4>Contact Information:
<TD><TEXTAREA NAME="con_info" COLS=40 ROWS=3></TEXTAREA>
</TABLE>
<INPUT TYPE="SUBMIT" VALUE="PLACE RESERVE">
<INPUT TYPE="RESET" VALUE="CLEAR FORM">
</FORM>
</BODY>
</HTML>
```

This example shows an abbreviated form of coding in which the table tags are not expressed as tag pairs. This way of coding works, so use it to save yourself lots of additional typing.

A working version of this script can be found on the CD-ROM in the PERL folder under 9–3.pl.

PERL PROGRAM TO HANDLE THE MATERIAL RESERVE/HOLD FORM

```perl
#! usr/local/bin/perl
push(@INC,"/data1/ip/iubks/cgi-bin/");
require ("cgi-lib.pl");
&ReadParse; print &PrintHeader;
#standard WWW based header

#check incoming data for dangerous characters
if ($in{'title'} =~ /[\\/\\^\\%\\@\\#\\*\\/\\\\ ] /)
     {print ("Invalid Character");
     die ( );}

     if ($in{'author'} =~ /\/\@\#\%\^/)
     {print ("Invalid Character");
     die ( );}

     if ($in{'material_type'} =~ /\/\@\#\%\^/)
     {print ("Invalid Character");
     die ( );}

     if ($in{'date'} =~ /\/\@\#\%\^/)
     {print ("Invalid Character");
     die ( );}

     if ($in{'user_name'} =~ /\/\@\#\%\^/)
     {print ("Invalid Character");
     die ( );}

     if ($in{'contact'} =~ /\/\@\#\%\^/)
     {print ("Invalid Character");
     die ( );}

     if ($in{'con_name'} =~ /\/\@\#\%\^/)
     {print ("Invalid Character");
     die ( );}

     if ($in{'call_number'} =~ /\/\@\#\%\^/)
     {print ("Invalid Character");
     die ( );}

#standard security, check the length of incoming variables before trying
to use them

if (length ($in{'title'}) > 200) {print ("Illegal command");

          die ( );}

if (length ($in{'author'}) > 200) {print ("Illegal command");

          die ( );}

if (length ($in{'material_type'}) > 200) {print ("Illegal command");

          die ( );}

if (length ($in{'date'}) > 200) {print ("Illegal command");

          die ( );}
```

```
if (length ($in{'user_name'}) > 200) {print ("Illegal command");
        die ( );}
if (length ($in{'contact'}) > 200) {print ("Illegal command");
        die ( );}
if (length ($in{'con_info'}) > 200) {print ("Illegal command");
        die ( );}
if (length ($in{'call_number'}) > 200) {print ("Illegal command");
        die ( );}

# read all variables into a list and store them, making it easier to access them in the program.

@user_vars[0] = $in{'title'};
@user_vars[1] = $in{'author'};
@user_vars[2] = $in{'material_type'};
@user_vars[3] = $in{'date'};
@user_vars[4] = $in{'user_name'};
@user_vars[5] = $in{'contact'};
@user_vars[6] = $in{'con_info'};
@user_vars[7] =$in{'call_number'};

#New stuff here, we are not going to open a file- instead we can send an e-mail message
#This line opens a mail message with the subject reserve request and is sent to the account
#paul@wccnt.lib.oh.us

open (MAIL, "\/usr/ucb/Mail -s \"Reserve Request\" paul\@wccnt.lib.oh.us");

#the following write information to the email message
print MAIL ("Title: @user_vars[0]\n");
print MAIL ("Author: @user_vars[1]\n");
print MAIL ("Format: @user_vars[2]\n");
print MAIL ("Date needed: @user_vars[3]\n");
print MAIL ("Requested by: @user_vars[4]\n");
print MAIL ("Prefer to be contacted by @user_vars[5]\n");
print MAIL ("Contact information: @user_vars[6]\n");

#close and send the email message
close (MAIL);

#Output a response to the user, in HTML

print ("<head><title>Reserve request submitted</title></head>");
print ("<body bgcolor=\"ffffff\">");
print ("<font size=5>Your reserve has been submitted.<br>");
print ("The library will contact you when your materials");
print ("have arrived.");
```

This program took the information submitted by a visitor and sent it, as an e-mail message to the library staff member responsible for placing holds on materials. To send e-mail directly from your PERL script use the following code:

```
open (MAIL, "path to mail program -s \"Subject Line \" "email address");
print MAIL ("Text to print in message");
close (MAIL);
```

Remember that each e-mail program, and the path to it, is slightly different. Consult your specific e-mail program documentation if you have problems sending e-mail from your PERL script. Never use the information submitted by a visitor in the e-mail address or subject lines of the message; doing so could compromise your Web server's security.

Leaving page 147 blank makes it possible for us to show you the interlibrary loan request form (page 148) on the page facing the HTML coding used to create it (page 149). The PERL coding that makes it functional follows on pages 150–151.

CREATING AN INTERLIBRARY LOAN (ILL) REQUEST FORM

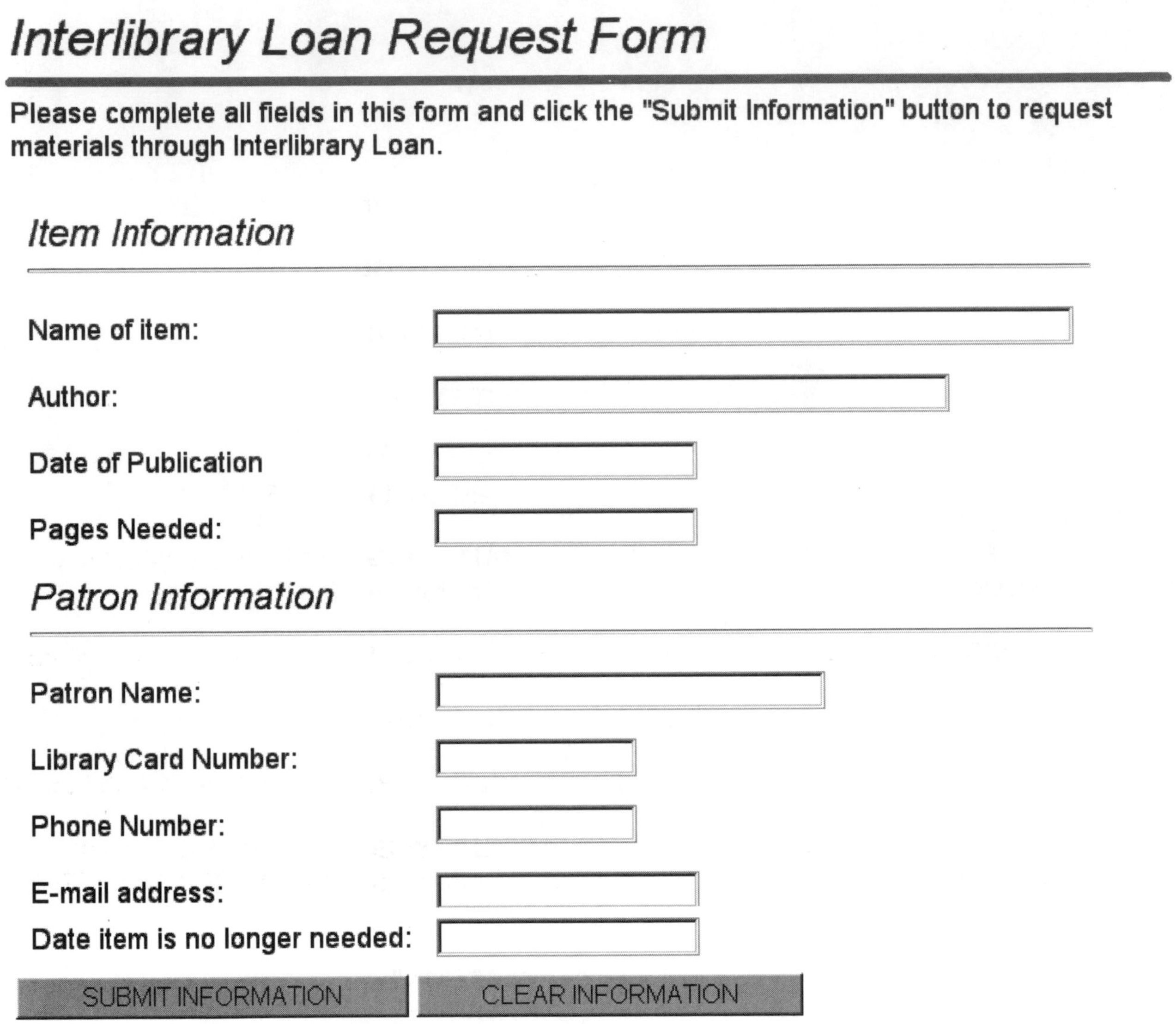

Interlibrary Loan Request Form

Please complete all fields in this form and click the "Submit Information" button to request materials through Interlibrary Loan.

Item Information

Name of item: [   ]

Author: [   ]

Date of Publication   [   ]

Pages Needed: [   ]

Patron Information

Patron Name: [   ]

Library Card Number: [   ]

Phone Number: [   ]

E-mail address: [   ]
Date item is no longer needed: [   ]

[SUBMIT INFORMATION]   [CLEAR INFORMATION]

Figure 9–4: Interlibrary Loan Request Form

ILL REQUEST FORM IN HTML

A working version of this form can be found on the CD-ROM in the HTML folder under 9–4.html.

```
<HTML>
<HEAD>
<TITLE>ILL Form</TITLE>
</HEAD>
<BODY BGCOLOR="FFFFFF">
<FONT SIZE=6>
<I>Interlibrary Loan Request Form</I>
<FONT>
<HR SIZE=6 NOSHADE><FONT SIZE=4>
```
Please complete all fields in this form and click the "Submit Information" button to request materials through Interlibrary Loan.
```
<FORM ACTION="http://www.yourserver.com" METHOD="GET">
<TABLE CELLPADDING=6>
<TR><TD COLSPAN=4><FONT SIZE=5><I>Item Information</I>
<HR>
<TR><TD><FONT SIZE=4>Name of item:<TD><INPUT TYPE="TEXT"
NAME="Item" SIZE=50>
<TR><TD><FONT SIZE=4>Author:<TD><INPUT TYPE="TEXT"NAME="Author" SIZE=40>
<TR><TD><FONT SIZE=4>Date of Publication:<TD><INPUT TYPE="TEXT"
NAME="Date_of_pub">
<TR><TD><FONT SIZE=4>Pages Needed:<TD><INPUT TYPE="TEXT"NAME="Pages">
<TR><TD COLSPAN=4><FONT SIZE=5><I>Patron Information<HR>
<HR>
<TR><TD><FONT SIZE=4>Patron Name:<TD><INPUT TYPE="TEXT" NAME="User_name"
SIZE=30>
<TR><TD><FONT SIZE=4>Library Card Number:<TD><INPUT TYPE="TEXT"
NAME="Card_number" SIZE=15>
<TR><TD><FONT SIZE=4>Phone Number:<TD><INPUT TYPE="TEXT" NAME="Phone"
SIZE=15>
<TR><TD><FONT SIZE=4>E-mail address:<TD><INPUT TYPE="TEXT" NAME="Email">
<TR><TD><FONT SIZE=4>Date item is no longer needed:<TD><INPUT TYPE="TEXT"
NAME="Need_date">
</TABLE></CENTER>
<INPUT TYPE="SUBMIT" VALUE="SUBMIT INFORMATION">
<INPUT TYPE="RESET" VALUE="CLEAR INFORMATION">
</FORM>
</BODY>
</HTML>
```

This example shows an abbreviated form of coding in which the table tags are not expressed as tag pairs. Coding this way works and can save you lots of additional typing.

A working version of this script can be found on the CD-ROM in the PERL folder under 9–4.pl.

PERL PROGRAM TO HANDLE THE ILL REQUEST

```perl
#! usr/local/bin/perl
push(@INC,"/data1/ip/iubks/cgi-bin/");
require ("cgi-lib.pl");
&ReadParse;
print &PrintHeader;

#standard WWW based header

#standard security, check the length of incoming variables before
#trying to use them

if (length ($in{'Item'})> 200) {print ("Illegal command");

        die ( );}

if (length ($in{'Author'}) > 200) {print ("Illegal command"); die ( );}

if (length ($in{'Date_of_pub'}) > 200) {print ("Illegal command");

        die ( );}

if (length ($in{'Pages'}) > 200) {print ("Illegal command");

        die ( );}

if (length ($in{'User_name'}) > 200) {print ("Illegal command");

        die ( );}

if (length ($in{'Card_number'}) > 200) {print ("Illegal command");

        die ( );}

if (length ($in{'Phone'}) > 200) {print ("Illegal command");

        die ( );}

if (length ($in{'Email'}) > 200) {print ("Illegal command");

        die ( );}

if (length ($in{'Need_date'}) > 200) {print ("Illegal command");

        die ( );}

# read all variables into a list and store them, making it easier to
#access them in the #program.

@user_vars[0] = $in{'Item'};
@user_vars[1] = $in{'Author'};
@user_vars[2] = $in{'Date_of_pub'};
@user_vars[3] = $in{'Pages'};
@user_vars[4] = $in{'User_name'};
@user_vars[5] = $in{'Card_number'};
@user_vars[6] = $in{'Phone'};
@user_vars[7] = $in{'Email'};
```

```perl
@user_vars[8] = $in{'Need_date'};

#pattern matching to ensure security, if data contains certain dangerous escape
#characters the program will stop

while ($cnt < 8)
    { if (@user_vars[$cnt] =~ /\!\@\#\%\^/)
            {print ("Illegal metacharacter, all uses logged.");
            open (FILE, ">>alert.txt");
            print FILE ("User from IP: $ENV{'REMOTE_ADDR'}\n");
            print FILE ("Host name: $ENV{'REMOTE_HOST'}\n");
            print FILE ("USER Browser: $ENV{'HTTP_USER_AGENT'}\n");
            print FILE ("QUERY: $ENV{'QUERY_STRING'}\n");
    close (FILE);
    die ( );
            }#end if statement
    $cnt ++;
    }#end while
## Send E-mail message ####
open (MAIL, "\/usr/ucb/Mail -s \"Reserve Request\" tjpaul@somewhere.org")
print MAIL ("Item: @user_vars[0]\n");
print MAIL ("Author: @user_vars[1]\n");
print MAIL ("Date of Pub.: @user_vars[2]\n");
print MAIL ("Pages @user_vars[3]\n");
print MAIL ("Requested by: @user_vars[4]\n");
print MAIL ("Card Number: @user_vars[5]\n");
print MAIL ("Phone: @user_vars[6]\n");
print MAIL ("Email: @user_vars[7]\n");
print MAIL ("Date needed by: @user_vars[8]\n");
close (MAIL);

#Output a response to the user, in HTML
print ("<HEAD><TITLE>ILL request submitted</TITLE></HEAD>");
print ("<BODY BGCOLOR=\"ffffff\">");
print ("<font size=5>Your request for Interlibrary Loan materials has been"); print
("submitted.<BR>");
print ("The library will contact you when your materials");
print ("have arrived.");
```

CREATING A LIBRARY CARD REGISTRATION FORM

Library Card Application

Applying for a library card is easy using the Web. Just follow the simple steps below:

- Complete all sections of this application form.
- Verify that all information is correct before clicking the "Submit" button.
- Click the "Submit" button.
- You can pick up your library card in three working days

Please note:

You can pick up your new library card at the main branch information desk during normal hours.
You will be required to present a photo ID.

Is this a new card, renewal, or replacement:	New ○ Renewal ○ Replacement ○
Last name:	
First name:	
Address:	
County of Residence:	
Phone:	
E-mail:	
Perfered contact:	E-mail ○ Phone ○ Postcard ○
Employer: (OPTIONAL)	
Work Phone: (OPTIONAL)	

I agree to comply with my library's policies and regulations. I agree to abide by the borrowing policies established by the Library Board of Trustees. I agree to replace or pay for the repair of all materials which are damaged while charged out to my card. I understand that violation of these polices can result in cancellation of my library privileges.

Clicking the apply button below signifies your agreement to the above. All information you supply is confidential and subject to verification.

Figure 9–5: Library Card Application Form

LIBRARY CARD REGISTRATION FORM IN HTML

A working version of this form can be found on the CD-ROM in the HTML folder under 9–5.html.

```
<HTML>
<HEAD>
<TITLE>Library Card Application Form</TITLE>
</HEAD>
<BODY BGCOLOR="FFFFFF">
<FONT SIZE=6><CENTER>Library Card Application </FONT>
<HR SIZE=6 NOSHADE>
<FORM ACTION="http://www.yourserver.com/cgi-bin/reserve.pl" METHOD="GET"> <TABLE
BORDER=2>
<TR><TD COLSPAN =2>Applying for a library card is easy using the Web. Just follow the simple
steps below:
<UL><l>
<LI>Complete all sections of this application form.
<LI>Verify that all information is correct before clicking the "Submit" button.
<LI>Click the "Submit" button.
<LI>You can pick up your library card in three working days
</l></UL>
<B>Please note:<P></B>
You can pick up your new library card at the main branch information desk during normal hours.
<BR>You will be required to present a photo ID.
<P>
<TR><TD><FONT SIZE=4>Is this a new card, renewal, or replacement:
<TD>New<INPUT TYPE="RADIO" NAME="c_type" VALUE="NEW">
Renewal<INPUT TYPE="RADIO" NAME="c_type" VALUE="RENEWAL">
Replacement<INPUT TYPE="RADIO" NAME="c_type" VALUE="REPLACEMENT">
<TR><TD><FONT SIZE=4>Last name: <TD><INPUT TYPE="TEXT" NAME="lname" SIZE=30>
<TR><TD><FONT SIZE=4>First name:<TD><INPUT TYPE="TEXT" NAME="fname">
<TR><TD><FONT SIZE=4>Address:<TD><TEXTAREA NAME="address" COLS=40 ROWS=3></
TEXTAREA>
<TR><TD><FONT SIZE=4>County of Residence:<TD><INPUT TYPE="TEXT"
NAME="county">
<TR><TD><FONT SIZE=4>Phone:<TD><INPUT TYPE="TEXT" NAME="phone">
<TR><TD><FONT SIZE=4>E-mail:<TD><INPUT TYPE="TEXT" NAME="email">
<TR><TD><FONT SIZE=4>Preferred contact: <TD>
E-mail <INPUT TYPE="RADIO" NAME="contact" VALUE="EMAIL">
Phone<INPUT TYPE="RADIO" NAME="contact" VALUE="PHONE">
Postcard<INPUT TYPE="RADIO" NAME="contact" VALUE="POST">
<TR><TD><FONT SIZE=4>Employer: </B>(OPTIONAL)<TD><INPUT TYPE="TEXT"
NAME="employ" SIZE=30>
<TR><TD><FONT SIZE=4>Work Phone:</B>(OPTIONAL)<TD><INPUT TYPE="TEXT"
NAME="wk_phone">
</TABLE></CENTER>
<HR SIZE=6 NOSHADE>
<FONT SIZE=4>
```

I agree to comply with my library's policies and regulations. I agree to abide by the borrowing policies established by the Library Board of Trustees. I agree to replace or pay for the repair of all mate-

rials which are damaged while charged out to my card. I understand that violation of these polices can result in cancellation of my library privileges.
\<P\>
Clicking the apply button below signifies your agreement to the above.
All information you supply is confidential and subject to verification.
\</FONT\>\<P\>
\<INPUT TYPE="SUBMIT" VALUE="APPLY"\>
\<INPUT TYPE="RESET" VALUE="CLEAR FORM"\>
\</FORM\>
\</BODY\>
\</HTML\>

This example shows an abbreviated form of coding in which the table tags are not expressed as tag pairs. This coding works and can save you lots of additional typing.

PERL PROGRAM TO HANDLE THE LIBRARY CARD REGISTRATION FORM

```perl
#! usr/local/bin/perl
push(@INC,"/data1/ip/iubks/cgi-bin/");
require ("cgi-lib.pl");
&ReadParse;
print &PrintHeader;
#standard WWW based header
```

A working version of this script can be found on the CD-ROM in the PERL folder under 9–5.pl.

```perl
#standard security, check the length of incoming variables before trying
to use them
if (length ($in{'c_type'}) > 200) {print ("Illegal command");
          die ( );}
if (length ($in{'lname'}) > 200) {print ("Illegal command");
          die ( );}
if (length ($in{'fname'}) > 200) {print ("Illegal command");
          die ( );}
if (length ($in{'address'}) > 200) {print ("Illegal command");
          die ( );}
if (length ($in{'county'}) > 200) {print ("Illegal command");
          die ( );}
if (length ($in{'phone'}) > 200) {print ("Illegal command");
          die ( );}
if (length ($in{'email'}) > 200) {print ("Illegal command");
          die ( );}
if (length ($in{'contact'}) > 200) {print ("Illegal command");
          die ( );}
if (length ($in{'employ'}) > 200) {print ("Illegal command");
          die ( );}
if (length ($in{'wk_phone'}) > 100) {print ("Illegal command");
          die ( );}

# read all variables into a list and store them, making it easier to
#access them in the #program.

@user_vars[0] = $in{'c_type'};
@user_vars[1] = $in{'lname'};
@user_vars[2] = $in{'fname'};
@user_vars[3] = $in{'address'};
@user_vars[4] = $in{'county'};
@user_vars[5] = $in{'phone'};
@user_vars[6] = $in{'email'};
@user_vars[7] = $in{'contact'};
@user_vars[8] = $in{'employ'};
@user_vars[9] = $in{'wk_phone'};
```

```
#pattern matching to ensure security, if data contains certain danger-
#ous escape characters the program will stop

while ($cnt < 9)
    {
    #check all fields to ensure that the user has completed to form
    if ($cnt != 6)
    {
            if (length(@user_vars[$cnt] )< 2)
                    {
                    print ("All fields must be completed to apply");
                    print ("for a library card. Please check your data;
                    print ("and try submitting again");
                    die ( );
                     }#end inner if statement
    }#end outer if statement
            if (@user_vars[$cnt] =~ /\!\@\#\%\^\/ )
                    {print ("Illegal metacharacter, all uses logged.");
                    open (FILE, ">>alert.txt");
                    print FILE ("User from IP: $ENV{'REMOTE_ADDR'}\n");
                    print FILE ("Host name: $ENV{'REMOTE_HOST'}\n");
                    print FILE ("USER Browser: $ENV{'HTTP_USER_AGENT'}\n");
                    print FILE ("QUERY: $ENV{'QUERY_STRING'}\n");
            close (FILE);           die ( );
            }#end if statement
    $cnt ++;
    }#end while

# Send email message
open (MAIL, "\/usr/ucb/Mail -s \"Library card application\"
jpaul\@somewhere.org");
print MAIL ("Type of library card: $in{'c_type'} \n");
print MAIL ("Last name: $in{'lname' }\n");
print MAIL ("First name: $in{'fname' }\n");
print MAIL ("Address $in{'address' }\n");
print MAIL ("County: $in{'county' }\n");
print MAIL ("Phone: $in{'phone' }\n");
print MAIL ("Email: $in{'email' }\n");
print MAIL ("Preferred Contact: $in{'contact' }\n");
print MAIL ("Employer: $in{'employ' }\n");
print MAIL ("Work phone: $in{'wk_phone'}\n");
close (MAIL);

# Provide output to the screen
print ("Thank you $in{'fname'}, your request for a library \n");
print ("card has been submitted. It will be reviewed by the library \n");
print ("and should be ready for you to pick up in three working days. \n");
print ("<BR><A HREF=\"http://www.somewhere.com\">Back to home</A>");
```

These four sample HTML documents/PERL scripts illustrate many of the concepts and techniques that were discussed in Chapters 2 and 8. All of the documents/scripts are fully functional and you should be able to modify them easily to meet the needs of your library.

WHAT YOU'VE LEARNED

Congratulations! You should now know enough about PERL and CGI programming to create successful CGI scripts. The last two chapters have taught you the basics of PERL and CGI programming including:

- scalar and array variables;
- receiving input from HTML forms;
- *for* and *while* loops;
- *if . . . else* tests;
- opening, reading and writing to files;
- sending e-mail from your PERL script;
- pattern matching and substitution; and
- many of the other functions that are part of PERL, including *print*, *grep*, and *length*.

Appendix A

A User-Friendly Glossary

GENERAL TERMS

Browser, Web
Another name for a Web client. Browsers contact Web servers, request information from them, and display that information to you in the way you want to see it. Common Web browsers are Netscape, Internet Explorer, and Lynx.

CERN (Centre Européen pour la Recherche Nucléaire)
Place where the World Wide Web project originated and the Web was developed.

Client, Web
Another name for a Web browser. Web clients contact Web servers, request information from them, and display that information to you in the way you want to see it.

Freeware
Free software available via the Net and obtainable via the Web or UNIX FTP.

FTP (File Transfer Protocol)
An Internet function that enables you to transfer files from one computer to another.

GIF (Graphic Image Format)
A color graphic file format developed by CompuServe for storing images. GIF files are often found on the Web because they efficiently compress graphic information. They can be identified by the .gif file extension.

Gopher

A tool developed at the University of Minnesota, that provided text- and menu-based access to Internet resources prior to the Web.

Graphical Browser

A browser program capable of displaying graphics, video, sounds, etc., in addition to text. Graphical browsers, such as Netscape and Internet Explorer, enable you to navigate the Web and the rest of the Internet using a mouse.

GUI (Graphical User Interface)

Software that hides the technical stuff. GUIs make using a computer application a matter of pulling down a menu or clicking on an icon. Windows is a common graphical user interface that hides complex DOS routines and makes running application software like word processors simple. Netscape and Internet Explorer are common Web graphical user interfaces that hide HTML tags, hypertext link structures, and make cruising the Web simple.

Home Page

1. The primary page of a Web site. 2. The place where you start exploring the Web when you start up your browser software.

HTTP (Hypertext Transport Protocol)

A program that enables your browser to communicate with a Web server, get a response from the server, and transfer the data requested back to your computer.

Hypertext

Text formatted with specific HTML coding that enables you to jump from one place on the Web to another.

Inline Image

Graphics that are part of a Web document and its HTML tagging. When you ask your browser to display a Web page that contains an inline image, it loads right along with the Web page text.

Internet

An international network of computer networks that communicate with each other using a common communication language (protocol) called TCP/IP.

Internet Address

The address of a computer on the Internet. Internet addresses can be expressed as numerals, called an IP address (e.g., 128.32.4.2) or as a series of letters, called a pseudonym address (e.g., oplin.lib.oh.us),

Internet Explorer (IE)

A popular graphical Web browser, created by Microsoft, that supports images, sound, and video in addition to text.

IP Address

A numerical expression of an Internet address (e.g., 199.18.159.1)

JPEG (Joint Photographic Experts Group)

A graphics file format and compression technique developed by the committee for which it is named. JPEG reduces the size of a graphics file by as much as 96 percent. They can be identified by the .jpeg file extension.

Link, Hypertext

A connection to another Web site or another part of the same site. Links appear on Web pages as differently colored, underlined, or highlighted text. Links can also be represented by a graphic button, picture, or be imbedded in an image map.

Lynx

A text-based Web browser developed at the University of Kansas. Although graphical Web browsers are common today, there are still a significant number of Web users with older equipment that does not support Windows or Mac system 7. These users usually access the Web via Lynx.

Mirror Site, Web

A "carbon copy" Web site that contains the same information as a popular site. Mirror sites help Web users access popular information by providing them with alternate Web sites.

MPEG (Motion Picture Experts Group)

A video file compression format developed by the group for which it is named. They can be identified by the .mpeg file extension.

Multimedia Document

A Web document that integrates text, graphics, sound, video, etc.

NCSA (National Center for Supercomputing Applications)

An organization, based at the University of Illinois, Champaign-Urbana, that developed many versions of Internet software, including the first graphical browser, Mosaic.

Netscape

A popular graphical Web browser that supports images, sound, and video in addition to text.

Port Number

A number that identifies where you can find specific Internet application programs on a server (e.g., http://guaraldi.cs.colostate.edu:2000). Port numbers let computers know where to find and access a particular resource.

Program

A piece of computer software.

Protocol

Specific rules (e.g., TCP/IP) that define how computers respond when communicating with each other and pass data to and from each other. If two computers use the same protocol they can "talk." If not, they can't.

Server

1. A computer that runs server software. 2. The software that allows one computer to offer services to another computer.

SGML (Standard Generalized Markup Language)

A standard for creating tagged documents that describe text, graphics, and other aspects of a document. HTML is a subset of SGML.

Shareware

Low cost software available on the Net that you can obtain via the Web or UNIX FTP. The folks who write shareware ask, but do not require, you to pay for the software you download after you download it. (It is proper netiquette to send the requested amount to the software author.)

TCP/IP (Transmission Control Protocol/Internet Protocol)

The protocol, or common "language," of the Internet that allows different computers and computer systems to communicate with each other.

Telnet

An Internet function that allows your computer to login to a remote computer and view its resources. You can telnet to Net resources using a Web browser by setting the URL to read, telnet://.

Text-Based Browser

A browser that does not display graphics or provide multimedia access. Lynx is the most common text-based browser.

URL (Uniform Resource Locator)

1. An Internet address expressed so that any Web browser can understand it. 2. What you type to get your Web browser to search for, connect to, and display a Web site (or other Net tool). 3. The information imbedded into a hypertext link that tells your browser which computer to connect to and which information to request from the server computer. 4. A way of citing a Web or other Internet resource.

Viewer

A separate application program you store on your computer along with your Web browser program. Viewers work along with browsers to display graphics, video, various text formats such as PDF. Newer browser versions come with selected viewers included as part of the browser software package.

Webmaster

The person in charge of the technical aspects of a Web site.

Web Page

A Web document that is displayed by your browser. Single Web pages are linked together to form a Web site.

Web Server

A computer that houses Web documents and that runs HTTP software in order to communicate and share information with Web clients.

Web Site

A series of organized Web pages, created by libraries, businesses, government agencies, groups, or individuals.

World Wide Web (The Web, WWW, W3)

A worldwide network of computers that provides hypertext/media links to a wide variety of Internet resources.

HTML TERMS

Align

An HTML attribute that allows you to place text or graphics in different places on a page. Depending on the tag, the align attribute will allow you to place text/graphics to the left, right, top, bottom, or center. Use it sparingly for greatest effect. Align can help you create a more sophisticated look to your Web page.

Anchor

Anchors in an HTML document indicate where a link is located. Anchors show both the start and end of a hypertext link.

Attribute

A unique quality that an HTML tag can take on. Attributes are added to HTML tags and specify special conditions for that tag.

Body

The tag pair that identifies and contains the text that will appear to a visitor on their computer screen.

Bulleted List

A list created by specific HTML tags, which displays list items identified by either a bullet, asterisk, or some other non-numerical graphic element.

CGI (Common Gateway Interface)

A standard where external programs, such as web-based forms, can access programs on Web servers. CGIs are often written in PERL, C, or Applescript languages. They are commonly used to process Web-based forms.

Checkbox

Small graphic elements created by the **CHECKBOX** attribute. Used in Web forms, checkboxes are small empty squares that when clicked on, display an **x** and select that item for inclusion on the form. Usually more than one checkbox can be selected per list.

Columns
Vertical arrangements of data cells within a Web-based table.

Coordinates
Numerical values that represent a section of a picture in an imagemap. Coordinates are included in imagemap links and make it possible for the link to locate the correct URL to connect to.

CSIM (Client-Side Image Map)
An imagemap that loads from a Web server onto a user's browser and accesses links using only the user's browser.

Element
The basic unit of an HTML document. Elements (also called text) are displayed inside tag pairs or followed by single tags (**<TITLE>**Library Web Page**</TITLE>**)

Forms
HTML pages that are capable of submitting data from visitors to a CGI program on a Web server. Forms are used for such things as keyword searching, suggesting book purchases, or providing patron feedback.

Frame Targeting
Links in one frame of an HTML document that when clicked on display information in a different frame.

Frames
HTML tags that create a Web page that displays more than one window on a visitor's computer screen. Each frame can display different content.

Header
HTML tags that structure Web page text and identify main topics and subtopics. Each header level displays text differently (e.g., bold, larger) so that you can create a hierarchical arrangement of information for visitors.

HTML (Hypertext Markup Language)
An organized system of tags used to describe and create World Wide Web documents. HTML tags assign text special meanings, and contain formatting instructions for browsers, as well as structuring hypertext links. HTML is a subset of SGML.

HTML Document
A document that begins with an **<HTML>** tag and ends with an **</HTML>** tag. Each HTML document has a unique name that ends with either the .html or .htm file extension.

HTML Editing Program

A program that simplifies the creation of HTML documents. HTML editors provide you with menu item or button choices for inserting HTML tags into text. They eliminate the need for you to type in HTML tags manually.

Imagemap

Images that have hypertext/media links imbedded in them. You can create imagemaps either by hand-plotting coordinates for links or by using simple map creation programs like *Mapedit*.

Mapedit

An easy-to-use imagemap creation program. (Available on the CD-ROM that accompanies this book.)

Navigational Frame

A frame, usually placed at the bottom or left-hand side of a framed Web page, which contains a table of contents or Web site information map.

Numbered List

A list created by specific HTML tags, which displays list items arranged hierarchically by number.

Radio Buttons

Small graphic elements created by the RADIO attribute. Used in Web forms, radio buttons are small empty circles that when clicked on, display a black dot and select that item for inclusion on the form. Usually only one radio button can be selected per list.

Resize

Characteristic of an HTML frame-based document that determines if a user will be able to alter the size of a particular frame.

Rows

Horizontal arrangements of data cells within a Web-based table.

Scrollable

Characteristic of an HTML frame-based document that determines if a user will have the ability to scroll through a document if necessary.

Server-Side Imagemap

An imagemap that is stored on a Web server. Each time a user clicks on a server-side imagemap, the request is sent to the Web server it is stored on. (Unlike a client-side imagemap that loads, and is accessed, from a user's browser.)

Tables

HTML tags that allow you to set up text and graphic information on a Web page in columns or rows of information.

Tag

Specific instructions placed around text to indicate how Web browsers should display the text or how Web browsers will handle the text; e.g., **\<B\>**Plumfield Library **\</B\>**).

Title

An HTML tag that identifies the unique title for each document. Often, the words you use in the **\<TITLE\>** tag become the text that displays when you bookmark that page.

PERL TERMS

\n

The new line escape character, equivalent to a carriage return.

\t\

The tag escape character.

Access Mode

Used when discussing PERL file operations. PERL is able to perform one of three actions on any file: read the file, write to the file, and append data to the file. These actions are known as access modes.

Append File Access Mode

PERL access mode that is capable of adding data to the end of the file.

Array Variable

A variable capable of storing multiple data elements or pieces of information.

Assigning Value to a Variable

The act of declaring a value, either alpha or numeric, that will be stored in a variable.

Comparison Operators

Mathematical operators used to compare values of two variables or other pieces of data.

==	Equal to
!=	Not equal to
<=	Less than or equal to
>=	Greater than or equal to
<	Less than
>	Greater than

Conditional Statements

Statements that allow you to test for a condition and branch to different parts of your program depending on the result.

Date Command

Displays the current time and date settings stored by the computer. This command is often used to add a time stamp to incoming data.

Die Function

This function causes your program to stop running. It is often used in conjunction with error and/or security checking procedures.

Element

A single piece of an array variable.

Else

Conditional statement used with *if* and *elsif* statements. An *else* statement executes only if the conditions being evaluated in all existing *if* and *elsif* statements are not met.

Elsif

Conditional statement used in conjunction with *if* and *else* statements. An *elsif* statement is only evaluated if the condition being tested by a prior *if* statement is not met. The *elsif* statement will always be evaluated after an *if* statement and before an *else* statement. This allows the program to test for multiple conditions.

Execute

Run a computer program.

Exit Condition

Condition that when met causes either a *for* or *while* loop to cease execution.

For Loop

A program loop that will execute at least once and repeat until the exit condition is met.

Grep Function

A basic PERL pattern matching function used to search for simple data structures.

Header

The first few lines of a PERL program that include the path statement, location of the CGI-BIN directory and other pieces of information a PERL program needs to operate properly.

If

A conditional statement that executes if a particular condition is met (e.g., If this is true then do this).

Initializing a Variable

Initial use of and assignment of value to a variable.

Interpreter

A special program that helps to convert the PERL code that you create into code that the computer can execute.

Length Function

Evaluates the length of a variable or an array element. The result of the length function will be the number of characters in the data structure examined.

Loops

Sections of code capable of executing one or more times.

Matched String

Set of characters that match a specified pattern.

Name

A unique label used to refer to any variable and/or form element.

Pattern Matching

PERL function that evaluates and compares data to a specified pattern. The general format for pattern matching is: *$variable =~ /pattern to be matched/*. The symbols below are used to enhance PERL's pattern matching abilities:

[ ]   Specify a range of characters to be matched
[^]   Specify a range of characters not to be matched
\d   Matches any digit
\D   Matches any non-digit
\w   Matches any word character
\W   Matches any non-word character
\s   Matches any white space
\S   Matches anything other than white space

PERL (Practical Extraction and Reporting Language)

A popular programming language well suited to developing CGI scripts.

Print Function

PERL function that prints text to the screen, a file, or an e-mail message.

Read File Access Mode

File access mode that allows the contents of a file to be read and stored in memory but not altered or appended.

Scalar Variable

A PERL data element capable of holding any one piece of information.

Script

A small computer program that requires an interpreter to run.

Substitution
Advanced PERL pattern matching operation that locates and replaces a specified piece of text in a variable.

Value
Text or data assigned to a variable.

Variable
A container in the computer's memory used to hold changeable information.

While Loops
A program loop that will only execute if a particular condition is true. This loop will continue to execute until the specified condition is no longer true.

Write to a File
Change the information stored in a file.

Write File Access Mode
File access mode that allows the contents of a file to be overwritten with new data.

Appendix B

Read More about It . . .

HTML

Aronson, Larry. *HTML 3.2 Manual of Style*. Emeryville, CA: Ziff-Davis, 1997.

Brown, Mark R. and Jerry Honeycutt. *HTML 3.2 Starter Kit*. Indianapolis, IN: QUE, 1997.

December, John and Mark Ginsburg. *HTML 3.2 and CGI Unleashed*. Indianapolis, IN: Sams.net, 1996.

Eddy, Sandra. *HTML in Plain English*. New York: MIS Press, 1997.

Grabowski, Ralph. *The Web Publisher's Illustrated Quick Reference*. New York: Springer, 1997.

Graham, Ian. *HTML Sourcebook*. 3rd ed. New York: J. Wiley, 1997.

Kidder, Gayle. *Official HTML Publishing for Netscape*. 2nd ed. Durham, NC: Ventana, 1997.

Lemay, Laura. *Teach Yourself Web Publishing with HTML 3.2 in 14 Days*. Indianapolis, IN: Sams.net, 1997.

Martin, Teresa A. *The Project Cool Guide to HTML*. New York: Wiley, 1997.

Oliver, Dick. *Teach Yourself HTML 3.2 in 24 Hours*. Indianapolis, IN: Sams.net, 1997.

Scharf, Dean. *HTML 3.2 Visual Quick Reference*. Indianapolis, IN: QUE, 1997.

Scott, Richard, et al. *HTML 3.2 Quickstart*. Emeryville, CA: Ziff-Davis, 1996.

Taylor, Dave. *Creating Cool HTML 3.2 Web Pages*. Foster City, CA: IDG, 1997.

Tennant, Roy. *Practical HTML: A Self-Paced Tutorial*. Berkeley, CA: Library Solutions Press, 1996.

HTML—URLs

Bare Bones Guide to HTML
http://werbach.com/barebones/

A Beginner's Guide to HTML
http://www.ncsa.uiuc.edu/General/Internet/WWW/HTMLPrimer.html

BrowserWatch
http://browserwatch.internet.com/

Composing Good HTML
http://www.cs.cmu.edu/~tilt/cgh/

How Do They Do That With HTML?
http://www.nashville.net/~carl/htmlguide

HTML: An Interactive Tutorial for Beginners
http://davesite.com/webstation/html/

HTML Bad Style Page
http://www.earth.com/bad-style/

HTML Goodies
http://www.htmlgoodies.com/

HTML Help
http://www.htmlhelp.com/

HTML Quick Reference
http://www.cc.ukans.edu/~acs/docs/other/HTML_quick.html

META Dictionary
http://vancouver-webpages.com/META/

ReallyBig.com
http://www.reallybig.com/

Soaring to Greater Knowledge
http://www.geocities.com/Heartland/Plains/8693/reference1.html

Wade's HTML Tutorial
http://arachnophobia.mit.edu/afs/athena/user/w/s/wsmart/WEB/HTMLtutor.html

Web Developer's Virtual Library
http://www.stars.com/

Web Mastery
http://www.hypernews.org/HyperNews/get/www/html/guides.html

Webmaster's Reference Library
http://www.webreference.com/

Web-O-Matic
http://www.geocities.com/SoHo/9272/webomat.html

Web Wonk: Net Tips for Writers and Designers
http://www.dsiegal.com/tips/index.html

HTML EDITING PROGRAMS

Davis, Phyllis. *Front Page 97 for Windows.* Berkeley, CA: Peachpit Press, 1997.

Graves, Steve. *Build Your Own Frontpage 97 Website.* Albany, NY: Coriolis, 1997.

Gray, Daniel. *Web Publishing with Adobe PageMill 2.* Research Triangle Park, NC: Ventana, 1997.

Langer, Maria. *PageMill2 for Macintosh.* Berkeley, CA: Peachpit Press, 1997.

Langer, Maria. *PageMill 2 for Windows.* Berkeley, CA: Peachpit Press, 1997.

Matthews, Martin S. *Web Publishing with Microsoft FrontPage97.* Berkeley, CA: Osborne, 1997.

McClelland, Deke, and John SanFilippo. *PageMill2 for Dummies.* Foster City, CA: IDG, 1997.

Parker, Elisabeth. *HotDog Pro for Windows.* Berkeley, CA: Peachpit Press. 1998.

Smith, Bud E. *Creating Cool PageMill 2.0 Web Pages.* Foster City, CA: IDG, 1996.

EDITING PROGRAMS—URLs

HTML Converters
http://www.hypernews.org/HyperNews/get/www/html/converters.html

HTML Converters
http://www.excite.com/computers_and_ internet/graphics/web_page_design/
html_converters/

HTML Converters
http://www.yahoo.com/Computers_and_Internet/Software/Internet/World_Wide_Web/
HTML_Converters/

HTML Editors
http://www.excite.com/computers_and_internet/graphics/web_page_design/html_editors/

HTML Editors
http://www.yahoo.com/Computers_and_Internet/Software/Internet/World_Wide_Web/
HTML_Editors/

HTML Editors and Converters
http://www.w3.org//Tools/

Mac/s Big List of HTML Editors
http://www.hypernews.org/HyperNews/get/www/html/editors.html

HTML VALIDATORS AND CHECKERS

Doctor HTML
http://www2.imagiware/com/RxHTML/

Validators and Checkers (Yahoo)
http://www.yahoo.com/Computers_and_Internet/Information_and_Documentation/
Data_Formats/HTML/Validation_and_Checkers/

WEB SITE DESIGN

Champelli, Lisa. *Neal-Schman Webmaster.* New York: Neal-Schuman, 1997.
Designing Interactive Web Sites. Indianapolis, IN: Hayden, 1997.
DiNucci, Darcy. *Elements of Web Design.* Berkeley, CA: Peachpit Press, 1997.
Gloor, Peter A. *Elements of Hypermedia Design.* Boston, MA: Birkhauser, 1997.
Horton, William, et al. *The Web Page Design Cookbook.* New York: J. Wiley, 1996.
Leary, Michael. *Web Designer's Guide to Typography.* Indianapolis, IN: Hayden, 1997.
Metz, Ray E. and Gail Junion-Metz. *Using the World Wide Web and Creating Home Pages.* New York: Neal-Schuman, 1997.
Niederst, Jennifer. *Designing for the Web: Getting Started in a New Medium.* Sebastopol, CA: O'Reilly, 1996.
Parker, Roger C. *Web Design and DTP for Dummies.* Foster City, CA: IDG, 1997.
Schmeiser, Lisa. *Web Design Templates Sourcebook.* Indianapolis, IN: New Riders, 1997.
Siegal, David. *Creating Killer Web Sites.* 2nd ed. Indianapolis, IN: Hayden, 1997.
Waters, Crystal. *Universal Web Design.* Indianapolis, IN: New Riders, 1997.
Weinschenk, Susan. *GUI Design Essentials.* New York: Wiley, 1997.

WEB SITE DESIGN—URLs

Accessible Web Page Design
http://weber.u.washington.edu/~doit/Resources/web-design.html

Best Viewed with Any Browser
http://server.berkeley.edu/~cdaveb/anybrowser.html

Guide to Web Style
http://www.sun.com/styleguide/

Usable Web
http://usabelweb.com/

Web Design Guidelines for Public Libraries
http://web0.tiac.net/users/mpl/guidelines.html

Web Design for Librarians
http://scc01.rutgers.edu/SCCHome/web.htm

Yale C/AIM WWW Style Manual
http://info.med.yale.edu/caim/manual/index.html

GRAPHICS

LeMay, Laura. *Graphics and Web Page Design.* Indianapolis, IN: Sams.net, 1996.
LeWinter, Renee and Cynthia L. Baron. *Web Animation for Dummies.* Foster City, CA: IDG, 1997.
McCanna, Laurie. *Creating Great Web Graphics.* 2nd ed. New York: MIS Press, 1997.
Richards, Linda. *Web Graphics for Dummies.* Foster City, CA: IDG, 1997.
Tittel, Ed. *Web Graphics Sourcebook.* New York: Wiley, 1997.

Webster, Timothy. *Web Designer's Guide to Graphics.* Indianapolis, IN: Hayden, 1997.

Weinman, Lynda. *Deconstructing Web Graphics.* Indianapolis, IN: New Riders, 1996.

Weinman, Lynda. *Designing Web Graphics.* Indianapolis, IN: New Riders, 1996.

Weinman, Lynda. *Designing Web Graphics.2.* Indianapolis, IN: New Riders, 1997.

Weinman, Lynda. *Preparing Web Graphics.* Indianapolis, IN: New Riders, 1997.

Weinman, Lynda and Bruce Heavin. *Coloring Web Graphics.* Indianapolis, IN: New Riders, 1996.

Wodaski, Ron. *Web Graphics Bible.* Foster City, CA: IDG, 1997.

GRAPHICS—URLs

Animation and Graphics 4 Your Website
http://www.bellsnwhistles.com/

Preparing Graphics for the Web
http://www.servtech.com/public/dougg/graphics/

IMAGEMAPS

Imagemap Guides & Tutorials
http://www.cris.com/~automata/tutorial.shtml

Imagemap Help Page
http://www.ihip.com/

Imagemap Tutorial
http://hoohoo.ncsa.uiuc.edu/docs/tutorials/imagemapping.html

Kaspar's Image Map Tutorial
http://www.personal.psu.edu/users/k/x/kxs156/tut1.htm

Mapedit
http://www.boutell.com/mapedit/

FRAMES

Teague, Jason Cranford. *How to Program HTML Frames.* Emeryville, CA: Ziff-Davis, 1997.

FORMS

Carlos' Forms Tutorial
http://robot0.ge.uiuc.edu/~carlosp/cs317/cft.html

HTML Form Testing Home Page
http://server3.pa-x.dec.com/nsl/formtest/home.html

Web Communications HTML Forms Tutorial
http://www.webcom.com/~webcom/html/tutor/forms/

PERL AND CGI SCRIPTS

Asbury, Stephen. *CGI How-To: the Definitive Scripting Problem Solver.* Corte Madera, CA: Waite Group Press, 1996.

Foghlu, Michael. *PERL5 Quick Reference.* Indianapolis, IN: QUE, 1996.

Gundavaram, Shishir. *CGI Programming on the World Wide Web.* Sebastopol, CA: O'Reilly, 1996.

Hermann, Eric. Teach *Yourself CGI Programming with PERL5 in a Week.* 2nd ed. Indianapolis, IN: Sams.net, 1997.

Kabir, Mohammed J. *CGI Primer Plus for Windows.* Corte Madera, CA: Waite Group, 1996.

Lines, Stephen. *How to Program CGI with PERL5.0.* Emeryville, CA: Ziff-Davis, 1996.

Middleton, Bill, et al. *Web Programming with PERL5.* Indianapolis, IN: Sams.net, 1997.

Neuss, Christian. *The Webmaster's Handbook: PERL Power for Your Web Server.* Boston, MA: Thompson, 1996.

Niles, Robert. *CGI by Example.* Indianapolis, IN: QUE, 1996.

Patchett, Craig. *CGI/PERL Cookbook.* New York: Wiley, 1998.

Schwartz, Randal L. and Tom Christiansen. *Learning PERL.* Sebastopol, CA: O'Reilly, 1997.

Sol, Selena and Gunther Birznieks. *Instant Web Scripts with CGI-PERL.* New York: M&T Books, 1996.

Till, David. *Teach Yourself PERL5 in 21 Days.* 2nd ed. Indianapolis, IN: Sams.net, 1996.

Tittel, Ed. *CGI Bible.* Foster City, CA: IDG, 1996.

Weil, Bob and Chris Baron. *Drag 'n Drop CGI: Enhance Your Website without Programming.* Reading, MA: Addison-Wesley, 1997.

Wong, Clinton. *Web Client Programming with PERL.* Sebastopol, CA: O'Reilly, 1997.

PERL AND CGI SCRIPTS—URLs

ABC Tutorial on CGI
http://lpage.com/cgiexample.html

CGI Archive
http://www.technotrade.com/cgi/

CGI-LIB.PL Homepage
http://cgi-lib.stanford.edu/cgi-lib/

Common Gateway Interface
http://hoohoo.ncsa.uiuc.edu/cgi/

How to Write a CGI Program
http://www.csclub.uwaterloo.ca/u/mlvanbie/cgisec/

How to Write CGI-BIN Scripts
http://www.catt.ncsu.edu/projects/perl/index.html

Matt's Script Archive
http://www.worldwidemart.com/scripts/

Selena Sol's Public Domain CGI Script Library
http://www.extropia.com/

Appendix C

HTML Equivalent Characters

For information on how to use equivalent characters see Chapter 2.

GENERAL SYMBOLS

quotation mark	&# 34;	&quot;
ampersand	&# 38;	&amp;
less than sign	&# 60;	&lt;
greater than sign	&# 62;	&gt;
vertical bar	&#124;	&brvbar;
degree sign	&#176;	&deg;
multiplication symbol	&#215;	&times;
division symbol	&$247;	&divide;
plus or minus symbol	&#177;	&plusmn;
copyright symbol	&#169;	&copy;
registered trademark	&#174;	&reg;
paragraph symbol	&#182;	&para;

CURRENCY SYMBOLS

Cent sign	&#162;	&cent;
Pound sterling sign	&#163;	&pound;
Yen sign	&#165;	&yen;

NUMBERS

1/4	&#188;	&frac12;
3/4	&#190;	&frac34;
superscript 1	&#185;	&sup1;
superscript 2	&#178;	&sup2;
superscript 3	&#179;	&sup3;

FOREIGN LANGUAGE DIACRITICAL MARKS

umlaut	&#168;	&uml;
acute	&#180;	&acute;
cedilla	&#184;	&cedil;
grave	&# 96;	&grave;
inverted question mark	&#191;	&iquest;
inverted exclamation pt.	&#161;	&iexcl;
tilde	&#126;	&tilde;

LETTERS WITH DIACRITICAL MARKS OVER THEM

capital A with acute	&#193;	&Aacute;
small a with acute	&#225;	&aacute;
capital A with grave	&#192;	&Agrave;
small a with grave	&#224;	&agrave;
capital A with circumflex	&#194;	&Acirc;
small a with circumflex	&#226;	&acirc;
capital A with umlaut	&#196;	&Auml;
small a with umlaut	&#228;	&auml;
capital A with tilde	&#195;	&Atilde;
small a with tilde	&#227;	&atilde;
capital A with ring	&#197;	&Aring;
small a with ring	&#229;	&aring;
capital AE	&#198;	&Aelig;
small ae	&#230;	&aelig;
capital C with cedilla	&#199;	&Ccedil;
small c with cedilla	&#231;	&ccedil;
capital E with acute	&#201;	&Eacute;
small e with acute	&#233;	&eacute;
capital E with grave	&#200;	&Egrave;
small e with grave	&#232;	&egrave;
capital E with circumflex	&#202;	&Ecirc;
small e with circumflex	&#230;	&ecirc;
capital E with umlaut	&#203;	&Euml;
small e with umlaut	&#235;	&euml;
capital I with acute	&#205;	&Iacute;

small i with acute	&#237;	&iacute;
capital I with grave	&#204;	&Igrave;
small i with grave	&#236;	&igrave;
capital I with circumflex	&#206;	&Icirc;
small i with circumflex	&#238;	&icirc;
capital O with grave	&#210;	&Ograve;
small o with grave	&#242;	&ograve;
capital O with circumflex	&#212;	&Ocirc;
small o with circumflex	&#244;	&ocirc;
capital O with umlaut	&#214;	&Ouml;
small o with umlaut	&#246;	&ouml;
capital O with slash	&#216;	&Oslash;
small o with slash	&#248;	&oslash;
capital U with acute	&#218;	&Uacute;
small u with acute	&#250;	&uacute;
capital U with umlaut	&#220;	&Uuml;
small u with umlaut	&#252;	&uuml;
capital Y with acute	&#221;	&Yacute;
small y with acute	&#253;	&yacute;
small y with umlaut	&#255;	&yuml;

Appendix D

Hexadecimal Colors

This list of colors will help you to choose browser-safe hexadecimal color values for text, links, and background for your Web pages. (For a description of how to set up colored text, links in HTML; see Chapter 2.) Some of the colors in this list clearly went into a specific color group; others, like pink, purple, or the blue greens, were placed in the color grouping closest to the base color. How the colors display on the Web will depend on a visitor's monitor, monitor color setting, and even the browser they use. It is important, therefore, that you experiment with different colors. When you find one you like, check out how it looks using both VGA and super VGA monitor settings, and by viewing it using both PC and MacIntosh browsers. This list is arranged by color and number/letter values.

YELLOWS

FFCC00 – light gold
FFFFCC – light yellow
FFFF99 – light yellow
FFFF66 – light yellow
FFFF33 – medium yellow
FFCC33 – dark gold
FFFF00 – dark yellow

ORANGES

FF9900 – light rust
FF9933 – light yellow orange
FF9966 – light orange
FFCC66 – light salmon
FFCC99 – light salmon
FF6600 – medium yellow orange
FF6633 – medium orange
993300 – dark rust
993333 – dark rust
CC3300 – dark orange
FF3300 – dark yellow orange

PINK, LIGHT

FF9999 – pale pink
FF99CC – pale pink
FF99FF – pale pink
FFCCFF – pink
FFCCCC – pink
FF6699 – fuchsia
FF66CC – fuchsia
FF66FF – fuchsia

PINK, MEDIUM

CC0066 – pink
CC3399 – pink
CC3366 – pink
CC6699 – magenta
FF00CC – fuchsia
FF00FF – purple pink
FF33CC – fuchsia
FF33FF – fuchsia

PINK, DARK

990066 – purple pink
990099 – purple pink
CC0099 – purple pink
FF0066 – pink
FF3399 – hot pink
FF0099 – dark pink

RED, MEDIUM

FF6666 – red orange
CC0000 – red
CC0033 – cherry red
CC3333 – orange red
CC6666 – brown red
FF0000 – red
FF0033 – red
FF3333 – orange red

RED, DARK

660000 – deep red
660033 – very dark red
990000 – red
990033 – cherry red
FF3366 – cherry red

GREEN, PALE

99CC99 – blue green
99CC66 – green
99FFCC – blue green
99FF99 – green
99FFFF – blue green
CCFFFF – blue green
CCFFCC – green
99FF33 – yellow green
99FF66 – green
CCFF99 – yellow green
CCFF66 – yellow green
CCCC33 – yellow green
CCCC66 – khaki

GREEN, LIGHT

00FF00 – green
00FF33 – green
00FF66 – green
00FFCC – aqua
33CCCC – aqua
33FF00 – yellow green
33FF33 – yellow green

33FFCC – aqua
66CC00 – green
66CC33 – green
66CC66 – green
66CC99 – green
66FF00 – yellow green
66FF33 – yellow green
66FF66 – yellow green
66FF99 – green
66FFCC – blue green
66FFFF – blue green
99CC00 – yellow green
99CC33 – yellow green
99FF00 – yellow green
CCCC00 – yellow green
CCFF00 – yellow green
CCFF33 – yellow green

GREEN, MEDIUM

009900 – green
009933 – green
009966 – green
00CC00 – green
00CC33 – green
00CC66 – green
00CC99 – blue green
00FF99 – green
339900 – green
339933 – green
339966 – green
339999 – blue green
33CC00 – green
33CC33 – green
33CC66 – green
33CC99 – blue green
33FF66 – green
33FF99 – green
669900 – yellow green
669933 – yellow green
669966 – gray green
999900 – yellow green
999933 – yellow green

GREEN, DARK

003300 – forest
003333 – forest
006600 – green
006633 – green
0066CC – green
006666 – blue green
00CCCC – aqua
333300 – khaki
336600 – yellow green
336633 – green
336666 – blue green
666000 – khaki
999966 – gray green

BLUE, LIGHT

99CCFF – blue
00FFFF – turquoise
33FFFF – turquoise
6699FF – blue
66CCCC – turquoise
66CCFF – green blue
9999CC – blue

BLUE, MEDIUM

009999 – turquoise
0099CC – turquoise
3399CC – turquoise
3399FF – green blue
33CCFF – green blue
669999 – aqua
6699CC – blue

BLUE, DARK

000033 – navy blue
000066 – royal blue
000099 – royal blue
003366 – navy
0033CC – purple blue
006699 – teal

003399 – blue
00CCFF – green blue
0066CC – blue
0066FF – blue
0099FF – green blue
3366CC – blue
3366FF – purple blue
336699 – green blue

PURPLE, LIGHT

9999CC – purple
9999FF – lavender
CC99CC – red purple
CC99FF – red purple
CCCCFF – lavender

PURPLE, MEDIUM

9966FF – red purple
9966CC – purple
CC66CC – red purple
CC66FF – purple

PURPLE, DARK

0000CC – purple
0000FF – purple
0033FF – purple
330033 – black purple
330066 – red purple
330099 – purple
3300CC – red purple
3300FF – red purple
333366 – blue purple
333399 – blue purple
3333CC – red purple
3333FF – red purple
660066 – red purple
660099 – red purple
6600CC – purple
663366 – grape
663399 – grape
6633CC – grape
6633FF – grape

666699 – purple
6666CC – grape
6666FF – blue purple
6600FF – red purple
9900CC – red purple
9900FF – red purple
993366 – red purple
993399 – red purple
9933CC – red purple
9933FF – red purple
CC00CC – red purple
CC00FF – grape
CC33CC – red purple
CC33FF – red purple

BROWNS, TANS

CC9933 – light khaki
CC9966 – light brown
CC9999 – light purplish brown
CCCC99 – light tan
996600 – golden brown
996633 – medium brown
996666 – medium purplish brown
CC9900 – medium khaki
330000 – dark red brown
663300 – dark warm brown
663333 – dark purplish brown
CC6600 – dark khaki

GRAYS, WHITE AND BLACK

000000 – black
333333 – darkest gray
666666 – dark gray
999999 – medium gray
CCCCCC – light gray
FFFFFF – white

Appendix E

PERL Cheat Sheet

STANDARD PERL HEADER

```
#! usr/bin/perl
push(@INC,"/usr/WWW/httpd/public/cgi-bin");
require ("cgi-lib.pl");
&ReadParse;
print &PrintHeader;
```

PRINT STATEMENT

Format: *print ("Text to print");*

Sample: *print ("Hello world");*

VARIABLES

Scalar–*$var_name*

Array–*@var_name*

GREP FUNCTION

Format: *@found = grep (/search pattern/, @list_to_be_searched);*

Sample: *@matched_list = grep (/Brad Kent/, @patrons);*

LENGTH FUNCTION

Format: *length (variable to be examined);*

Sample: *length ($name);*

IF STATEMENTS

Format: *if (condition is true)*
{do this ;}

Sample: *if ($x < 23)*
{print ("The number is too low");}

IF . . . ELSE STATEMENTS

Format: *if (condition is true)*
{do this;}
else {do something else;}

Sample: *if ($a < 18)*
{print ("The number is too low");}
else {print ("Thank you for the input");}

IF . . . ELSIF . . . ELSE

Format: *if (condition is true)*
{do this;}
elsif (another condition is true)
{do something;}
else {do something else;}

Sample: *if ($a < 18)*
{print ("The number is too low");}
elsif ($a > 29)
{print ("The number is too high");}
else {print ("Thank you for the input");}

COMPARISON OPERATORS

==	Equal to
<=	Less than or equal to
>=	Greater than or equal to
<	Less than
>	Greater than
!=	Not equal to

WHILE LOOPS

Format:
while (exit condition)
{
Code to do something, may be as long as you like.
}

Sample:
while ($cnt < $a)
{
print ("The count is $cnt");
$cnt++;
}

FOR LOOPS

Format:
for (initialize variable; exit condition; loop counter)
{
code... . . . .
}

Sample:
for ($x = 1; $x < 10; $x++)
{
print ("Hello World \n");
}

OPENING FILE IN READ MODE

Format:
open (reference name, "filename");

Sample:
open (FILE, "readme.txt");

OPENING FILE IN WRITE MODE

Format: *open (reference name, ">filename");*

Sample: *open (FILE, ">readme.txt");*

OPENING FILE IN APPEND MODE

Format: *open (reference name, ">>filename");*

Sample: *open (FILE, ">>readme.txt");*

CLOSING FILES

Format: *close (reference name);*

Sample: *close (FILE);*

READING DATA FROM A FILE

Format: *open (reference name, "filename");*
                                 @storage variable = <reference name>;
                                 close (reference name);

Sample: *open (FILE, "my_file.txt");*
                                 @whole_file = <FILE>;
                                 close (FILE);

WRITING TEXT TO A FILE

Format: *open (reference name, ">filename");*
                                 print FILE("text to write to the file");
                                 close (reference name);

Sample: *open (FILE, ">my_file.txt");*
                                 print FILE("hello world");
                                 close (FILE);

APPENDING DATA TO A FILE

Format: *open (reference name, ">>filename");*
                                 print FILE("text to append to the file");
                                 close (reference name);

Sample:	*open (FILE, ">my_file.txt");* *print FILE("hello world");* *close (FILE);*

DIE FUNCTION

die ( );

PATTERN MATCHING

Format:	*$variable to be searched =~ /pattern to look for/;*
Sample:	*$user_name =~ /Joe Smith/;*

SPECIAL PATTERN MATCHING SYMBOLS

[ ]	Allows you to specify a range of characters to be matched. */B[ae]ll/ This matches either the word ball or bell.*
[^]	All characters EXCEPT those following the caret are matched. */[^ABC]/ This matches any letter other than A, B, or C.*
\d	Matches any digit
\D	Anything not a digit (letters and symbols)
\w	Any word character, includes numbers and letters but not punctuation or white space
\W	Any non-word character
\s	Matches white space
\S	Matches anything that is not white space

SUBSTITUTION

Format:	*$variable to be searched =~ s/pattern to replace/replacement pattern/;*
Sample:	*$user_name =~ s/Joe/Tim/;*

DATA FROM AN HTML FORM

Format: *$in{'form_element_name'};*

DATE COMMAND

Format: *'date'*

Sample: *print ("The time is: 'date'");*

INDEX

About the Authors

Gail Junion-Metz is president of Information Age Consultants. For the last five years she has been traveling around the United States and Canada teaching librarians and teachers about the Internet. Gail is the author of *K-12 Resources on the Internet* (2nd ed.) published by Library Solutions Press (1997), which was selected as one of this year's best professional books by *Library Journal*. She is co-author of *Using the World Wide Web and Creating Homepages*, published by Neal-Schuman. Gail also writes a monthly Net column for *School Library Journal* entitled "Surf For." Gail has an MA in Library Science from the University of Wisconsin. She has been a librarian at Indiana University, Cleveland State University, and the University of Rochester.

Brad Stephens is technology coordinator for NOLA Regional Library System. He has extensive experience in systems design and implementation, library automation, application programming, UNIX administration, TCP/IP networking, and computer security. Brad has an MLS from Indiana University. During his six years as a librarian, he has worked with a variety of automated systems. He has also trained staff and served as a consultant for many academic, public, and special libraries.